From Liberator to Dictator

From Liberator to Dictator

**An insider's account of Robert Mugabe's
descent into tyranny**

MICHAEL AURET

 davidphilip

Published in 2009 in southern Africa by David Philip Publishers,
an imprint of New Africa Books (Pty) Ltd,
99 Garfield Road, Claremont 7700, South Africa

www.newafricabooks.co.za

ISBN: 978-0-86486-731-5

Editor: James McFarlane
Text design and layout: Claudine Willatt-Bate
Proofreader: Lindsay Norman
Cover design: Nic Jooste, Comet Design
Cover photograph of Robert Mugabe: Paul Weinberg/South Photographs/
africanpictures.net

Printed and bound in South Africa by SED Printing Solutions

Contents

Preface

Part of the reason for writing this book was for me to try to gain some understanding of how so many of us so gravely misconstrued the situation in Zimbabwe once independence had been achieved. How was it possible that so serious an error of judgement could have been made by so many people, in the world, not only in Zimbabwe?

The book was started when I left Zimbabwe, the country of my birth, because by then I had realised that there was little hope that either a political or an economic solution was likely within the foreseeable future. I had come to understand that the hope that we had had was based on 'white' thinking; was based on our own assessment of how the 'blacks' saw us, and our need to hang on to a lifestyle, a countryside, a nationality, indeed an entirety of life that we so loved.

In 1980 we hoped that the black Zimbabweans would forgive and forget the contempt in which we had held them for so long, the indignities we had heaped on them, the lack of respect we had for the culture and customs of the people. We hoped that perhaps, against all that, they would weigh the development, the health and education, the communication facilities and the expertise we had brought, and find it at least pragmatic to allow us to stay, and most of all to allow us to keep the land we had occupied over the 90 years of the existence of the colony.

Almost exactly a year before independence, I was with the only real 'expert' on Zimbabwe I have known, one Patrick Galvin, a diminutive priest from Clara in Ireland who held a PhD in Anthropology and who had been studying the people he ministered to in Zimbabwe – he had learnt their language, culture and customs over the forty years he had lived in the country. I asked him what he thought would happen when the war was over, when the majority had taken over the government? His reply was, 'In time they will destroy everything white and rebuild it in their own way.' I pooh-poohed that thought as it was clear that no one would ever destroy so developed an infrastructure or economy. He answered, 'I'm not talking about infrastructure or buildings, I'm talking about white thinking, white attitudes and white domination. They will certainly attempt to rid themselves of that.'

Well, independence came – and that miracle of 'reconciliation'. I was vindicated, we were to stay. It took just twenty years for the truth of Pat's prophetic statement to emerge and begin to be realised. However, in the modern world, that kind of retribution is no longer possible. States cannot survive alone (Mugabe should have learned that from the UDI debacle) and crimes against humanity are no longer tolerated. So Mugabe, faced with the possibility of standing before the International Court of Justice if he lost control of the country, built the fences he considered necessary to safeguard himself and those many of his cronies who were as guilty as he.

Now, some years after I started writing, those fences are under serious attack. The people of Zimbabwe have chosen a new champion, the Movement for Democratic Change, a party which, despite its own internal difficulty, could lead the country through the minefield of negotiations with Mugabe and his ilk to a new beginning. Perhaps, someday soon, the people of Zimbabwe will be able to start the rebuilding and to know at last peace again. Much will remain to be done, however, before the recovery is complete, and, as hope burgeons in the hearts of those many Zimbabweans, in the diaspora and at home, I keep firmly in my mind the fact that while Mugabe and his minions are part of the equation, that hope will be tempered by the knowledge that there is little moral conscience among them, and perhaps they have another chapter to write before they succumb to the pressure of their neighbours and the world.

MTH Auret
August 2008

Foreword

The transformation of Robert Mugabe from a hero and international symbol for African freedom to a villain and an international outcast has been a depressing spectacle to witness. The change would not have been so tragic were it confined to the travails of a single individual and not the wholesale destruction of one of the most promising countries on the continent. From a liberation war hero, Robert Mugabe has effectively transformed himself into one of the most despicable dictators Africa has ever known. Mugabe has so tarnished his legacy that history will certainly judge him harshly.

If Mugabe had stepped down from office in the mid-1990s he might have been forgiven for some of the excesses of his rule and continued to be revered as Zimbabwe's founding father. His seminal policy of reconciliation did much to stabilise a hitherto racially polarised nation. The bloat was that in his single-minded pursuit of one-party rule the hand of reconciliation and unity was never extended to the Ndebele people of the western part of the country, who constituted the bulk of support for ZAPU (led by arch-rival Joshua Nkomo). It was an inauspicious beginning. The subsequent massacres of the Ndebele under *Gukurahundi* should have alerted people to Mugabe's quest for absolute power.

His first ten years in power must surely be seen as partial positive on the social and economic fronts. He expanded education and health facilities in areas not immediately affected by the early political disturbances. Agriculture also benefited from expansion of agricultural extension services to peasant farmers, which resulted in increased output of crops such as maize, cotton and tobacco.

Sadly, the successes scored in the first decade of Mugabe's rule have been systematically reversed by the policies pursued from 1998 to 2008. Central to this change in Mugabe has been the desire to hold onto power at all costs. Mugabe changed not because he wanted to reclaim land from the whites and defend Zimbabwe's sovereignty but because his political power was threatened – beginning in 1998, when veterans of the liberation struggle stood up to voice their concern that they had not benefited from independence while it was clear that Mugabe and the rest of the political leadership had. From then on, Zimbabwe was on the road to dictatorship.

Michael Auret's book is one man's journey from having believed in the ideals of Mugabe's early years to a complete metamorphosis in the man and these ideals. This is a book that will have many people wishing they had written their own account of how they misjudged Mr. Robert Mugabe. Mugabe remains an enigma, and not even his closest comrades – if there are any – know the man.

Mugabe had all of us fooled for one reason or other and at different times. He made each of us believe he was one thing when in fact he was something else. For example, during Zimbabwe's liberation struggle many believed he was a Marxist-Leninist and a terrorist in the mould of China's Mao Ze Dong. And yet, when he assumed office as Prime Minister of Zimbabwe in 1980, he proved to be nothing more than a pragmatic nationalist.

However, this side of him lasted for less than three years, for the *Gukurahundi* massacres showed him to be a callous megalomaniac. While claiming to be a socialist, his economic policies of plunder and primitive accumulation enriched only those closest to him in his administration. His brief flirtation with socialism was half-hearted and was soon abandoned in preference for prescriptions from the Bretton Woods twins. And even this phase did not last long.

Left-leaning University of Zimbabwe academics such as Dr Shadrack Gutto and Professor Kempton Makamure became enemies of the state merely for pointing out that the ZANU (PF) government was paying lip service to socialism. They had taken Mugabe at his word when he said he was a Socialist-Marxist. Kenyan-born Gutto was eventually hounded out of Zimbabwe, while Makamure found himself in and out of police detention, with both men accused of instigating student unrest at the university.

On the other hand, people like Rhodesian rebel prime minister Ian Smith and his ilk were convinced that Mugabe was a communist, leading white Zimbabweans to emigrate in droves for fear of the nationalisation of their properties. In the late 1980s and early 1990s many returned to Zimbabwe, from South Africa, Australia, New Zealand and the UK, when they thought they had misjudged Mugabe. And they were soon trapped when Mugabe felt his power threatened and launched a bloody land-grab and a state-sponsored terror that subverted private property.

Like most dictators, Mugabe has revealed only glimpses of his inner self and has avoided the close bonds of friendship that might betray his vulnerabilities to the larger world. And consistent with all dictators, all he has done has been directed at retaining political power at all costs. There is no consistent behavioral pattern that can be charted, except the single goal of maintaining absolute power.

Just like Mike Auret, I was taken in by Mugabe. In fact, I can confess that Robert Mugabe used to be my hero. At university, when I was vice-president of the Student Representative Council, I remember how proud I was when he came to visit us. I lined up to shake his hand in the Senior Common Room, and it was a moment I cherished.

At that time I was also the president of ZAPU on campus and my admiration of Mugabe, the president of ZANU, was unforgivable in the eyes of my fellow activists. His party had practised genocide in Matabeleland and the Midlands, which were ZAPU strongholds. Ordinarily, I should have hated this man.

In fact, were it not for my mother's influence, my natural instincts were to support Robert Mugabe instead of Joshua Nkomo, a man adored by my politically active mother. To me, Mugabe had the qualities of a modern African leader. I admired the way he spoke, his manner of thought, his vision. I looked forward to when he addressed the nation, and marvelled at how he fired such strong sentiments of patriotism and nationalism.

As I travelled the world, I was proud to be Zimbabwean, and especially proud that Mugabe was my president. He had restored the dignity that the race-based policies of Ian Smith had taken away from black Zimbabweans. Zimbabwe was African, independent and free; Mugabe was my man, and I never missed an opportunity to gloat.

How things have changed. Zimbabwe, the former breadbasket of the region, is now an economic basket case. Life expectancy has plummeted, and more and more people have abandoned the country. The constitution, the legislature and all other vital national institutions have been undermined, solely in the service of one man. He has personalised the police, army and security services and rendered Parliament useless. A man who could have been a Nelson Mandela – a figurehead for Africa – has instead destroyed people's lives and dreams. He has devastated a jewel of a nation. In pursuit of personal benefit, he has become a monster who clings on to power only because he can.

A few years ago, when I was visiting Bulawayo for my brother's wedding, my passport was seized. I was essentially a prisoner in my own country, and I had to go to court to get my passport back. More recently, the government tried to revoke my citizenship, and for three months I was a stateless person. My mother is Zimbabwean; I was born in Zimbabwe; and I lived there for the first four decades of my life. In 1994, I received an award as Zimbabwean editor of the year. But the government said that, because my father was born in Zambia, I was not Zimbabwean. However, I suspect that the real reason was that Mugabe regarded me as one of his enemies because I run the only two remaining independent newspapers left in the country. Fortunately, I was able to win the court case and got my citizenship back.

Mugabe has assaulted and poisoned our national pride and psyche, and it will take us a long time to get back to where we were at independence in 1980. He has turned our hopes into despair. The great expectations that political freedom held out in 1980 have been turned into a long nightmare. We have lost our pride and dignity as a people. Our hopes and dreams as a nation have been held hostage to Mugabe's steely determination to stay in power until he drops dead.

Just like Mike Auret, I have never been able to explain how different Mugabe is behind closed doors and when he speaks in public. I have met with Mugabe as part of a group of editors on at least two occasions, and each time I walked away thinking 'what a great man'. I found him engaged and informed and was convinced that it was the people around him who were to blame for the mess that the country is in. I also got the impression that he cared and had a generous spirit. I never, in any of these meetings, detected a cruel streak or an unkind word. And yet in public his language is undisciplined and fails to set a leadership benchmark in decorum. But then two meetings would never enable me to make a fair character assessment of anybody.

Surely leadership must be about setting an example, holding colleagues accountable and taking responsibility for actions and decisions taken? Mugabe has failed to set an example of good leadership and has failed to hold those around him accountable. In fact, most of them know that unless you threaten him directly Mugabe will allow you to do whatever you please with impunity – hence the mismanagement and rampant corruption.

Leadership is also about being big enough to say 'I am sorry' when things go wrong. Not once has Mugabe taken responsibility for his decisions and the actions of those around him. With Mugabe the buck stops with everybody else but him. He takes no responsibility for the mess that the country is in. The British and the Americans and their puppets in the MDC are to blame. According to him, inflation is the fault of the business community, not anything his government has done. And soon after independence, it was all the fault of Joshua Nkomo and the dissidents.

After his government destroyed homes and businesses of over 700 000 poor people during Operation Murambatsvina, Mugabe did not see fit to apologise to Zimbabweans. He did not apologise to the victims of *Gukurahundi*, except to call this a 'moment of madness'. Most elections in Zimbabwe have been violent, with loss of life and destruction of property, and not once has Mugabe stood up to condemn this abominable behaviour. As a result, he is responsible for a culture of intolerance where violence is perceived as the only way of settling political differences. Mugabe has presided over the pervasion of our norms and value system and this will take a long time to fix.

We have all misjudged Mugabe because we assumed that he was a democrat concerned with the well-being of his people. We assumed that he cherished the principles that fueled our heroic liberation struggle – justice, equality and human rights. Indeed, we assumed that Mugabe was interested in leaving a legacy and working to ensure that Zimbabwe and Zimbabweans were better off than when he took over from Ian Smith. It has taken us more than 28 years to realise that, to him, politics is about Robert Mugabe – no more, no less. Indeed, strip out all the eloquent anti-imperialist and anti-Western rhetoric and you find an old man desperate to cling to power. The fear of life without political power has driven Mugabe to trash the same principles that saw him lead the liberation struggle.

Sadly, I have also come to realise that there was a lot that was wrong with the liberation struggle, which explains many problems we have experienced over the past 28 years. It was a murderous struggle in which the end justified the means. Intimidation, murder, torture and total disregard of human rights were the hallmark of the war against the Smith regime. As evidenced by the orgy of violence leading up to and following the 2008 presidential election run-off, the ghosts of the liberation struggle have come back to haunt us. It is these same ghosts that were responsible for the *Gukurahundi* massacres, Murambatsvina, the violent land-grab and state-sponsored election violence.

Those who knew Mugabe during the struggle say that we are witnessing the real Mugabe. Whatever the case is, we should draw a line in the sand and say to ourselves never again shall one man hold the hopes and dreams of our nation to ransom. And we will do that by ensuring that the new Zimbabwe is underwritten by a human rights-based constitution. National institutions must be sacrosanct and take precedence over the interests of the political leadership of the day.

Trevor Ncube
Chief Executive Officer
Mail & Guardian Media

Acknowledgements

In the first instance, I wish to acknowledge with great admiration the many people, black and white, whose courage and determination have served Zimbabwe so well; those many who are still trying desperately to bring hope and succour to the suffering citizens of the country; those who are working in exile, as it were, to bring a welcome change to the political and economic situation there; and those who have died in the struggle.

I would like to say a great 'thank-you' to my family, and especially to my wife, Di, who suffered through the long, drawn-out production process and assisted immeasurably with corrections to both text and memory, with editing and with encouragement both to complete the work and to find a publisher. She and our son Michael spent a long week editing, correcting cajoling and threatening, which finally paid off. The rest of the family have listened to my regurgitation of the story many times without complaining and have given great encouragement.

Thanks also to Trevor Ncube, a most courageous journalist, for taking the time in his very busy life to write the Foreword.

I wish to extend my thanks to New Africa Books, and in particular to Alfred LeMaitre, for accepting and publishing this effort; and to James McFarlane, the copy editor, for his patience and care. Thanks also to Kay Sayce, who helped me with the early editing and encouraged me to continue, and many thanks to John Cooper for his early encouragement and edit.

M.T.H. Auret
Cloghan, Co. Offaly
Eire

Prologue

Robert Mugabe is a man of great strength and power. I had heard of his control in the detention camp, where he demanded rigorous programmes of physical fitness for all the detainees, banned smoking and ensured that anyone with any education would teach those with less. In detention, with the tragedy that touched him at the death of his only son (at that time), he showed his strength and his determination to achieve the end of colonisation and domination by the 'white settlers'.

I am one of those 'white settlers'. I would never have called myself that until it became clear that the majority of the people in Zimbabwe considered anyone of a Rhodesian background to be an interloper. By the time Robert Mugabe came to power in 1980 I had spent 10 years in the Federal Army and 12 years farming, and in 1978 I had been invited to take up the post of Organising Secretary to the Justice and Peace Commission (JPC) in the Catholic Bishops' Conference. I later became the Chairperson of the JPC, which had become the country's main human rights organisation, which I served for the following 19 years.

Listening to Mugabe's 1980 election speech I was convinced that at last the country we so loved would find peace and stability. It was a remarkable speech of reconciliation:

> If yesterday I fought you as an enemy, today you have become a friend and an ally with the same national interest, loyalty, rights and duties as myself ...

Mugabe came to power with a great roar of approval from thousands of voices. Loud ululation continued as the Catholic Archbishop of Harare blessed the new flag and, as it was raised for the first time, silence fell and Mugabe took his oath of office. The Prime Minister's speech on Independence Day, 18 April 1980, emphasised the new government's policy of forgiveness and reconciliation, and included an invitation to Zimbabweans of all races to live and work together in harmony in this new era.

> The wrongs of the past must now stand forgiven and forgotten … It could never be a correct justification that because whites oppressed us yesterday when they had power, the blacks must oppress them today because they have power. An evil remains an evil whether practised by white against black or black against white.

Later, Father Pius Ncube (Archbishop Ncube 1997) was to describe these speeches as the most Christian speeches he had ever heard from a politician.

Less than two years later, however, Mugabe had set his dogs of war, the North Korean-trained Fifth Brigade onto the civilian population of Matabeleland, in an attempt to rid himself of political opposition. This brigade, commonly known as Gukurahundi, or the 'rain that washes away the chaff', set about their task – detaining, raping, torturing and killing many thousands of people; the exact number may never be known, but estimates place the number between 10 000 and 15 000 dead.

When questioned about the activities of the Fifth Brigade, he responded vehemently 'we have to deal with this problem quite ruthlessly, don't cry if your relatives get killed in the process.' Later he stressed, 'when men and women provide food for the dissidents, when we get there we eradicate them. We do not differentiate who we fight because we can't tell who is a dissident and who is not.'

I was to experience this dichotomy in Mugabe slowly and painfully over the next two decades.

People say that opposites attract. There are perhaps few people more opposite than a malign dictator and a human rights worker, one black and the other white. Yet my relationship with Robert Mugabe was, in my mind at least, a close one. Towards the end of the 1970s and in the first months of 1980 I developed a great respect for the man and, as the relationship grew, that respect grew into something closely related to love. I believed in him and, while disillusionment has well and truly set in now, it is a relationship that I find difficult to explain, even to myself, for although there was much interaction on a political level, we met on a social level only a few times. I met him on several occasions about very troubling issues. I met him socially, when serious issues were not discussed and human feelings were given space. From the beginning I had a great feeling for him and what I believed was his love for the country and its people.

Was Mugabe a man of peace and reconciliation, or violence and vengeance? Was he ever a man of peace and democracy? If not, how did we err so seriously in our judgement of him?

Before Independence

PART ONE

CHAPTER 1

Grappling with Change

It is difficult to understand where it all started, but in my mind the connection between Mugabe and the elder Kabila, late president of the Democratic Republic of the Congo, has echoes of the savagery and anarchy that marked the Belgian Congo at the time of its independence in 1960.

I was a young subaltern in the Northern Rhodesia Regiment at the time of the Belgian rout from the Congo. I watched the beginning and the unfolding of that great African tragedy, which continues into this century. Since 1960, the journey has been a long learning experience of a white African trying to understand why so much has gone wrong in Africa. The impact of the Congo on me was profound, bringing with it the confusion which always arose when I heard of 'liberation forces' destroying people and the infrastructure meant to benefit them.

At the time of the Congo debacle, the first battalion of the Northern Rhodesia Regiment (1NRR), a black regiment led by white officers and part of the army of the Federation of Rhodesia and Nyasaland,[1] had been sent to the Congo border near the small town of Kipushi, a mining town less than a mile from the border and about 20 miles south of Elizabethville. We watched the huge exodus of white Belgians leaving, most in a state of abject terror and mourning the loss of loved ones. Most of them were well armed and many were deeply traumatised, perhaps none more so than three Belgian nuns who had been raped when their convent was looted and destroyed. These good Sisters had given their lives to the well-being of the people of the Congo and they could not comprehend the tragedy. The extraordinary violence of this period is a reflection of almost a century of extremely cruel and grossly exploitive occupation by Belgium, in a colonial system that was driven by greed and the violent subjugation of the people.

Part of our task while on the border was to confiscate weapons from people coming across the border. When the exercise was over we had many thousands of weapons, including shotguns, rifles and handguns. The time spent there also included a meeting with Moise Tshombe, then the leader of Katanga Province, a part of the Congo that wished to secede from the rest of the country, and either go it alone or join the Federation of Rhodesia and Nyasaland. This connection with the Federation led Tshombe to travel south several times through our station at Kipushi, which by this time had been reduced to company strength. On one of the return trips he was forced to stop at the camp because his car, an enormous Lincoln Continental, had developed a leak in the petrol tank which I was able to repair – at least well enough for him to reach home – by closing the hole in the tank with soap. It was the first time I had ever seen a car with a telephone in it. I was impressed. I and my company commander, John Hickman, later General Officer Commanding of the Rhodesian Army, were able to communicate with Tshombe and his party in schoolboy French that caused some mirth but certainly broke the ice. Tshombe struck me as a decent, honourable man whose intentions in attempting to break away from the Congo were in the interests of the people of Katanga.

The United Nations (UN), however, saw it differently and, controversially, prevented the secession. By this time, Tshombe's forces were losing the battle against the UN forces, but they were determined to continue the struggle. Part of that struggle was launched from the base at Kipushi where the Katangese 'air force' – at that time comprising an elderly Messerschmitt and a Piper Cherokee – occasionally used our airstrip, taking off in the early evening to do whatever damage it could to the Elizabethville airport that had been taken over by UN forces. The two pilots – Jan, a Belgian, and Peter, an Englishman – flew sorties from the airfield and occasionally

..... *The 'Officers' Mess', Kipushi, on the Congo border, 1960.*

had drinks in our 'Officers' Mess', a pole-and-thatch structure that gave us some protection from the heat.

The Congo refugees passed through Northern Rhodesia and into Southern Rhodesia before finding their way to Belgium. On their way through they were cared for by many people in both countries and they told the most horrifying stories of the atrocities committed against the colonisers, against missionaries and against one another after independence was granted. The anger of the people against the colonisers had exploded even more violently than that of the Mau Mau vengeance in Kenya only a few years earlier. This anger was to show itself again in Uganda when Idi Amin expelled the Asian community from that country and, much later, in Zimbabwe.

In central Africa in the late 1950s and early 1960s, because of the policies of the Federal government and the influence of Garfield Todd (later Sir Garfield), the former Prime Minister of Southern Rhodesia, racial attitudes among whites had begun to soften, particularly in Southern Rhodesia. Unhappily, the effect of the horror stories arriving with the Belgian refugees was to change all that, as racial attitudes hardened once again and fear of black government grew. The extreme violence of the conflict in the Congo was to lay the foundation for the many great difficulties and conflicts endured by the people of that nation up to the present time.

One of the tragedies of that time was the untimely death, in an aircraft accident, of Dag Hammarskjöld, the UN Secretary General, in September 1961. He was flying to Ndola in Northern Rhodesia for a meeting with

..... Dag Hammarskjöld,
UN Secretary
General at the time.

..... Carrying the Regimental Colour of
the Northern Rhodesia Regiment,
Tug Argan Barracks, Ndola.

Tshombe over the future of Katanga when his aircraft crashed in dense bush a few miles from the airport. A few days later I was privileged to command the guard of honour that escorted his body from the hearse to the aircraft at Ndola airport. Rumours abounded about how the aircraft came down, with some fingers pointing to the Federal authorities. However, the conclusion reached by both the Federal investigation team and the UN investigators was that the crash was the result of pilot error. Despite those findings, the rumours blaming the Federal Prime Minister, Sir Roy Welensky and the 'Rhodesians' continued for some years.

In February 1962, I was sent with five colleagues to serve for six weeks with various British Army units in Kenya, as part of an Officer Exchange Programme. For all of us it was the first time that we had visited other African countries and the journeys by Land Rover there and back were memorable. The incredible scenery, the wildlife in the Ngorongoro Crater Game Reserve, the first sight of Mount Kilimanjaro and the friendliness of the people made me understand why we white Africans so love the continent. At that time both Kenya and Tanganyika (later Tanzania) were expecting their independence fairly soon, but whereas there had been no conflict over the issue in Tanganyika, the violence of the Mau Mau uprising in Kenya was still very much in the minds of the people of all races there. There was also a hint of tension among the senior officers in the regiments to which we were attached for the six weeks. We had all been sent to different units and all experienced the same reticence when we began to discuss the situation in the Federation. It was only some time later that we heard that the British government was unsure about Welensky's reaction to the Monckton Commission Report recommending the break-up of the Federation.

While in Kenya I went with a platoon of men part of the way up Mount Kenya, through some of the territory that the Mau Mau had used as bases and I understood the enormous difficulties the British forces faced in trying to flush out the fighters of that organisation. Thick, almost impenetrable bamboo forest covered much of the slopes and I could see how nearly impossible it was to find anyone in that growth. But the British Army engineers, at least, kept their sense of humour; they had built a wooden bridge across a small stream on the mountainside and placed a carved wooden notice on it reading, 'Elephants are requested to cross in single file'. It seems that the elephants in Kenya could read, as the bridge was still standing many years later.

..... Percival's Bridge, on Mt. Kenya. The sign reads 'Elephants are requested to cross in single file'.

By this time, Harold Macmillan's 'winds of change'[2] were howling through Africa, and European countries with colonies in Africa were abdicating their responsibilities and disengaging in the quickest and least expensive way possible. In the Federation, nationalist forces of the individual countries were making themselves heard, with Dr Hastings Banda

– who had been practising medicine in Britain for 20 years – in Nyasaland, Kenneth Kaunda and Harry Nkumbula in Northern Rhodesia, and Joshua Nkomo in Southern Rhodesia all applying pressure on their respective governments, the Federal government and Britain to bring an end to the Federation and grant independence to their countries.

The army was called out on several occasions to help the police maintain order. On one such call-out I was witness to a tragedy in the tiny village of Kabompo, near the border with Angola. Kenneth Kaunda's United National Independence Party (UNIP) had been holding rallies in the area, causing unrest and disturbances. The police Mobile Unit had been sent in to make arrests in the area and my platoon was sent in as a back-up for them. Our base was on the west bank of the Zambezi River, which at that point was wide and deep and had to be crossed by ferry. The Mobile Unit crossed early one morning and arrested about 16 people. We watched the return journey and saw that there was some sort of disturbance on the ferry that caused it to capsize. There was some amusement when most of the police and prisoners were tossed into the water; the ferry was close to the river-bank and we were convinced that they would all simply wade ashore. Then, to our growing horror, it became clear that the people in the water were panicking and obviously in serious trouble. We ran down to the bank, some 500 yards, and when we reached it we learned that 13 prisoners and three policemen had not surfaced. I and several others immediately dived in to find them and I was amazed at how precipitous was the bank and how deep the water.

None of those who had gone down was saved. For days afterwards we patrolled the river searching for their bodies. On the second day a local fisherman recovered the bodies of a policeman and a prisoner, still handcuffed together. The policeman was white and by the time the bodies had been brought to the bank a very large and hostile crowd had developed. The crowd surrounded the bodies and threatened to hack the arm off the policeman to release the prisoner's body. The District Commissioner (DC) who was there remonstrated with the crowd, which was by that time very threatening. I had already formed my platoon into riot control formation when the DC, with enormous courage, walked into the mob, released the handcuffs and allowed the people to remove the body of the prisoner.

I was greatly affected by this tragic loss of life, partly because I knew the policemen who had died but also because of the great loss of life among the people who were beginning to show their desire for an end to colonialism and the attainment of self-determination. I was still firmly convinced that the Federation was good and was therefore angry with the nationalist politicians who wanted to see it ended. The other countries of the Federation were also experiencing political upheaval, and once the British Government had sent Lord Monckton to the Federation to gauge the situation, the end of that remarkable achievement was imminent.

In Southern Rhodesia in 1963, a new party, the Zimbabwe African National Union (ZANU) made its appearance, with the Reverend Ndabaningi Sithole breaking away from Joshua Nkomo's Zimbabwe African People's Union (ZAPU), the black political party that until then had been the sole representative of the black people of Southern Rhodesia. The extraordinary violence at the birth of ZANU was to set that party on its violent path to independence and its aftermath. In this way, the tribal bias of the two parties was emphasised.

The country had two major tribal or linguistic groups – the Shona (about 70% of the black population) and the Ndebele (about 20%), with the other 10% made up of Tonga, Venda, San and others. While the original nationalist party had previously embraced people of any tribal group, when Sithole broke away from ZAPU he took the Shona group with him, but the Ndebele remained loyal to Nkomo. When the parties divided, there was much violence in the high-density suburbs of Salisbury and Bulawayo and soldiers from the NRR were sent down to assist in maintaining order. In Salisbury, petrol-bombing the houses of people who remained loyal to ZAPU was the method ZANU chose to use to intimidate its opponents and to force them to change their allegiance. Much more would be seen of ZANU's violent proclivities in the years ahead.

Notes

1 The Federation of Rhodesia (i.e. Northern and Southern) and Nyasaland came into being in September 1953 after protracted negotiations with the British government. The joining of these three central African countries brought great economic growth to them and brought black Africans into the political arena. It lasted 10 years and ended in December 1963.

2 Harold Macmillan, the British Prime Minister at the time, said in a speech in Ghana, 'I recognise that the wind of change is blowing through Africa, but the emergence of African countries to nationhood represents a major new development in the world.' See Welensky, R. *4000 Days*. Collins, 1964, page 170.

CHAPTER 2

A Soldier's Conflict

In late 1961 and early 1962, the garrison at Kipushi was reduced to platoon strength, which meant that on two six-week tours of duty I was alone on the border with my platoon of about 30 men. Being without white companions, having meals with the troops and relaxing with them in the evenings caused me to begin to question my own racial attitudes and to understand that indeed these men had the same worries about wives and children that we had, they had the same raunchy humour as any other soldiers and bled the same colour when injured. It was altogether a confusing time in my heart and mind as it was difficult to adjust from the simple acceptance that black people were inferior, to the fact that they were not. This was the beginning of a long and sometimes tortuous process of change for me.

Kipushi also initiated another learning process – the moral rights and wrongs of the death penalty. Until then, the judicial killing of murderers was a matter of course; it happened everywhere and was not questioned, at least in my mind. However, while at Kipushi on one tour of duty, I decided to cross the border to the local mining club to have a drink and to watch a movie called *I Want to Live* about a woman, played by Susan Hayward, facing, and finally suffering, the death penalty. That film started me wondering about the morality of the death penalty although my thoughts on the matter crystallised only many years later when I came into contact with Amnesty International and its efforts to persuade countries to reject that irreversible ultimate penalty.

In 1962, while still in the army, I was introduced to politics for the first time. I was at the School of Infantry in Gwelo at the time, on a conversion course from the old .303 rifle to the new self-loading rifle (SLR) when Edgar Whitehead, Prime Minister of Southern Rhodesia, called for a referendum on the new constitutional proposals that would, for the first time, divide the country along racial lines. Normally, members of the armed forces were not allowed to take part in politics, but on one particular morning our course was interrupted by a call for all ranks to parade, and I was greatly angered when the Commander of the School of Infantry ordered us to vote in favour of the new proposals; I had already decided to vote against them. A small group known as the United Group led by Clifford du Pont (later President of Rhodesia) and one Ian Douglas Smith, had been formed to oppose the proposals. (It was the only time that I would agree with Smith on any political matter.) I worked for the group, albeit clandestinely, in a minor way while I was on the course and voted 'No' when the time came. However, the majority of white voters voted 'Yes' and the proposals became the 1962 Constitution of Southern Rhodesia. At that time only whites could vote.

African politics was interesting to white Rhodesians only from the point of view of maintaining control. Few whites understood the underlying political aspirations of the black Rhodesian which caused the unrest in the early 'sixties; but for black Rhodesians many very important processes were taking place. At this time the black nationalist leader was Joshua Nkomo. Nkomo, a sometime driver and carpenter had, as an adult, completed his secondary education, a social work diploma and finally a bachelor's degree in economics and sociology. He later became the leader of the Railway Workers' Union and a very popular political leader. Between 1953 and 1962 Joshua Nkomo led the Rhodesian Nationalists in parties under various titles. So the original party had been known as the African National Congress (ANC), this was followed by the National Democratic Party (NDP), then by the Zimbabwe African People's Union (ZAPU), which later became the People's Caretaker Council (PCC), and still later returned to ZAPU and finally to the Patriotic Front (ZAPU)

(PF (ZAPU)).Whenever a party was banned by government, the original ANC simply re-emerged under a different name. Initially Joshua Nkomo, *the* nationalist leader at this time, had agreed to the constitutional proposals. He had attended the 1961 Constitutional Conference at the invitation of Sir Edgar Whitehead and his party accepted the proposals in the first instance. Later, just before the referendum, he rescinded his agreement and spoke out strongly against the proposals, particularly in the south and west, perhaps to appease other African leaders.

While the 1962 referendum was not the first time I had used my vote, it was the first time I had felt really strongly about a political issue and the first time I felt the anger of political defeat. The experience gave me a taste for politics which I have never lost. I began to wonder if any of the voters had taken the time to understand what the constitutional proposals meant to the country in the long term and, indeed, if they cared. However, the 1962 Constitution was short lived and many changes were to occur between 1962 and the turn of the century, as you will see.

At the end of 1963, with the demise of the Federation of Rhodesia and Nyasaland, my service with the NRR also came to an end. The news of the break-up and the choices we had were brought to us in the NRR by the Federal Secretary for Defence, Sydney Sawyer; many years later, after the country had become Zimbabwe, I and his widow Eileen, a remarkable lady, became close friends and colleagues in the struggle for human rights and democracy. The armed forces of the Federation paraded together for the last time at a farewell parade for Sir Roy Welensky, the Federal Prime Minister, at Glamis Stadium in the Salisbury Show Grounds. Sir Roy was presented with a three-furrow plough and we saluted our Regimental Colour for the last time. It was an emotional occasion for all concerned. The political chicanery of the British Government over the break-up of the Federation,[1] combined with the hardening racial attitudes caused by the Belgian experience, had set Southern Rhodesia on the path to right-wing politics, the election of the Rhodesian Front government in December 1962, and civil war.

I returned to Southern Rhodesia and was posted to the newly formed

Rhodesian Light Infantry (RLI). As the inter-party violence continued in the townships, the RLI was called out to help the police in 'cordon and search' operations. I took part in two of these operations and they were my first experience of life in the 'townships' of Salisbury, which increased my growing confusion about my role as a soldier. I had grave misgivings about the violation of the people's right to privacy and freedom of movement. The townships had been designed as 'dormitory' areas for the workers in the city. While black domestic workers were allowed to live in the domestic servants' quarters built in the grounds of almost every white-owned house in Rhodesia, the factory and other city workers were accommodated in these dormitories – tiny brick and asbestos houses, often semi-detached and always very close together. They were not designed for family accommodation and workers' families were expected to remain in the 'reserves', often far from where the workers lived. This form of migrant labour caused untold harm to family structures, distorting the culture and contributing to the destruction of the inherent morality of the people.

After a year in the RLI, I was sent to the Headquarters of 2 Brigade (HQ 2 Bde) in Salisbury as the Military Intelligence Officer (MIO), a post that gave my father and siblings much cause for mirth over the level of intelligence needed to be an MIO. This position required me to travel widely in the country and I visited many areas I had never seen before. It truly was a very beautiful country and I would have been content to serve it without bearing arms.

In 1965, 2 Bde was on an exercise in the Zambezi valley, looking at the defence of Rhodesia in the face of attack from Zambia – probably, although we did not know it at the time, in preparation for the Rhodesian Declaration of Independence from Britain. While on that exercise, one of my former colleagues in the NRR came through our camp and told us of the Lumpa uprising in Zambia. It had been put down by President Kaunda's troops and I was told that the mortar platoon of the former 1 NRR had been the first into action against these innocent people. This news was most disturbing for me, as my last post in the NRR had been to command that mortar platoon and to bring the platoon up to date with a new 81 mm mortar that was replacing the old 3" mortar. I had formed a close relationship with the men, and now these same men whom I had trained had been used to kill the inoffensive and defenceless Lumpa people. What was more disturbing for me was that I had known the Lumpa, the followers of Alice Lenshina (she was a visionary and formerly a Catholic), as hardworking, devout, sober people who refused to take part in any political activity. This refusal had obviously displeased Kaunda who required all Zambians to join UNIP. His forces therefore stirred up revolt among the Lumpa people and then destroyed them. My reaction was deeper than just distress at what had happened. As a Catholic, convinced and practising, a deep feeling of unease occupied my mind, once again, concerning my role as a soldier. 'Can it be right to bear arms of war, to train people to kill, no matter what the circumstances?' That question began to occupy my mind more and more.

Many years later I was to meet President Kenneth Kaunda at State House in Lusaka, Zambia, and I found him a gentle person who seemed to have a great concern for his people. He appeared to be humble and likeable and yet he had sanctioned the violence which had silenced the Lumpa people in order to achieve 'political unity' in Zambia. The same contradiction was later to become apparent in Mugabe.

Notes

1   The duplicity of the British Government over the Federation experience is well documented in Sir Roy Welensky's *4000 Days* (Collins 1964).

CHAPTER 3

Growing Awareness

At the break-up of the Federation in 1963, independence was promised to both Northern Rhodesia and Nyasaland, but was withheld from Southern Rhodesia as that country had been self-governing since 1923, but still had a racial minority government and appeared to have little intention of changing that situation in the foreseeable future. Winston Field and Ian Smith were part of the team that negotiated the terms of the dissolution of the Federation and the disposal of its assets, but they failed to win from Britain the promise of independence.

Subsequently there was pressure on Winston Field to threaten Britain with the government's intention to declare Rhodesia independent unilaterally if Britain would not grant it. However, Field was loath to take such a step and that led to his being ousted by Ian Smith. The new Prime Minister then negotiated with the Wilson government. Wilson consulted the tribal chiefs of Rhodesia, but what emerged from that consultation was the 'sixth principle': No Independence Before Majority African Rule, more commonly referred to as NIBMAR. Negotiations continued in 1965 until November of that year, when Smith and his cabinet declared Rhodesia independent. What followed was inevitable.

In 1963 a split occurred in the nationalist party. Several prominent black leaders had lost faith in Nkomo after he had agreed to the 1961 constitutional proposals, and despite his later retraction of that support, Nkomo never again led the entire black population in their political struggles. A new party emerged from this split; born in the house of Enos Nkala, when Ndabaningi Sithole, Leopold Takawira, Robert Mugabe and Nkala himself met and decided to establish the Zimbabwe African National Union (ZANU), under the leadership of the Rev Ndabaningi Sithole, with a young man named Robert Mugabe as its Secretary-General. Leopold Takawira was the Vice-President and Nkala Treasurer.

Robert Mugabe, born in 1924, had lived and was educated at Kutama, which is a Jesuit Mission. He did extremely well at his studies under the tuition of Fr O'Hea, finishing with a Primary School Teaching Diploma. He taught at various schools in Rhodesia, including Dadaya, which was run by Garfield and Grace Todd, missionaries from New Zealand. He was raised a Catholic and his mother Bona[1] ensured that at least while he was at home he practised his faith. In years to come he was to complete several degrees, the first of which was at Fort Hare, where he was introduced to nationalist politics. In 1958 he travelled to Ghana where he met and married his wife Sally. On his return to Rhodesia he joined the NDP under Nkomo as the publicity secretary. As the Secretary-General of the newly formed ZANU he was known to be a powerful speaker. In 1964 he was arrested for calling a piece of proposed legislation 'the legalisation of murder'. He was sentenced to a year in prison, but on his release he was redetained along with other nationalists and was to remain in detention for more than 10 years.

The nationalist parties (ZAPU and ZANU) were outraged by the illegal step Smith and his government had taken and considered that there was no longer any chance that a political solution could be found. They accordingly called on Britain to take immediate and even military action to stop Smith, and to regain British control; this Britain consistently refused to do. Both nationalist parties, however, had already sent young people out of the country for military training and had sent party officials to Britain and other European countries to gain support and finance for their party activities. Ndabaningi Sithole had already approached the People's Republic of China for military assistance and Joshua Nkomo was wooing the Eastern Europeans in the Soviet bloc.

The end of 1965 was also the end of my military career. When Smith declared independence, an act that became famous as 'UDI' – the Unilateral

Declaration of Independence – he made the announcement to the world in a lunchtime broadcast. I heard the announcement as I was on my way by car to the Military College in Pretoria to attend a course in interrogation on 11 November 1965. I was stunned and indeed frightened by the step he had taken and what it might mean to the country in which my parents, my siblings, my children and I had all been born and loved so well. I also knew that I could not serve a government that had taken so blatantly illegal a step. The media reports of what was happening in Rhodesia in the following few days crystallised my decision to leave the army.

On my return from Pretoria I accordingly submitted my resignation. I had sworn allegiance to Queen Elizabeth II on joining the army and despite the fact that Smith's duplicity kept her as Head of State, although he had overthrown her government's rule in the colony, I was unable to reconcile the new situation with my oath of allegiance. It was also clear from the tone of Rhodesian Front politics that we could no longer expect any *rapprochement* with black Rhodesian politics. I decided to join my father on a farm he managed in the Belingwe area, south-west of Shabani.

In 1966 Harold Wilson took the case of Rhodesia to the United Nations and as a result mandatory sanctions were applied against the Smith government and the country. The government then initiated several measures to counter the effects of sanctions, with remarkable success in the early years. Petrol rationing was introduced, with ration coupons, reminiscent of the situation in World War II; import and export controls were put in place; currency exchange was very carefully managed; and generally the people tightened their belts. Among the more beneficial effects of these sanctions was the diversification of agriculture. From a fairly laissez-faire life on the farms, farmers were required to become far more efficient producers and to move away from the traditional production of tobacco, maize and cattle into new crops including sugar, cotton, oil seeds, and sheep and goat production. Indeed the farmers became, and for many years remained, the mainstay of the economy.

Belingwe is a small village about 120 miles south-west of Gwelo and the same distance south-east of Bulawayo, a dry area ideally suited to cattle farming. It is also an area where gold, asbestos and jade have been mined. The roads were atrocious; the low level bridges often flooded in the wet season and the rivers would dry out immediately after the season ended. The village consisted of a post office, government offices, staff houses, a police camp, a government hospital, a small primary school for white children, a hotel attached to the all-purpose store and a somewhat dilapidated sports clubhouse. Nearby was the 'African location' for the black workers and their families. The farm itself was approximately 15 miles from the village, lying south of Mount Belingwe, with its peak and ridge forming the northern boundary of the farm.

When we moved to the farm Di (Diana) and I had been married for 10 years and we had three children aged five, four and three, a happy handful indeed. I took over as manager of this mainly cattle enterprise when my father retired in 1968, and we moved into the main house – a beautiful, gracious old Rhodesian home, with huge rooms, high ceilings and large windows overlooking the valley in the south and the mountain in the north. The following 12 years were spent on this farm and for at least the next six years it was to give the family joy, peace and security – and time to reflect.

The white farming community in Belingwe was much the same as in all small communities – friendly and helpful neighbours. We had the added advantage of my parents having been well loved in Belingwe, and we were accepted readily. Our relaxation was generally at the local mine club, the Vanguard Mine where we played tennis, saw the occasional movie and had Christmas celebrations. Civil servants in the village changed quite regularly but always seemed to fit in well and we had many enjoyable times. As the years went by and our time in the area lengthened so our relationship with our neighbours, both black and white, strengthened.

Being the farm manager meant that I had a staff of workers responsible to me and for whom I was, in turn, responsible. The relationships I had had with my troops in the army now stood me in good stead on the farm, as I was able to relate easily to the workers (more commonly referred to as 'the gang') and to develop in them great loyalty and a positive work ethic. That process was another learning time for me, assisted by several people whose knowledge and advice were to be very important to me in the future.

The first of these was a Professor Silberbauer, a South African race and labour relations expert. I attended a seminar he gave for farmers in Bulawayo. He spoke frankly about black/white relations at a time when South Africa was deeply divided racially and Rhodesia was moving in that direction. In the field of labour and management in particular, he pointed out the errors into which white management often fell because of their lack of knowledge and understanding of the culture and customs of the workers. For me, the gem of the seminar was the explanation he gave of an issue that had worried me since starting work on the farm. Each morning I went out to start the gang off on their day's labour and was puzzled by the fact that they did not greet me, although our relationship was generally good. Silberbauer told us that whereas in white culture the junior person always greeted the senior first, in black culture the opposite was true – the junior did not speak until spoken to. So if we wished to be greeted by our workers, we must greet them first. When I tried that the following morning on the farm I was thrilled by the response I got to my greeting. That little gesture made a big difference to my relations with the workforce.

The second person to assist in this field of racial understanding was a Catholic priest, Patrick Galvin, an Irishman who had joined the Swiss Bethlehem Missionary Society, and who was in 1968 the Mission Superior of Mutuzukwe Mission in the tribal area, south of the farm (in the Belingwe reserve). Being Catholic farmers in Belingwe meant that we were served by the mission priest from Mutuzukwe Mission, which meant that every alternate Sunday Fr Patrick said Mass at 6.00 pm for us, his third that day, and then he could sleep over and spend Monday with us. The priests stationed at the mission – there were two or three over the years we were there – were all from the Swiss Bethlehem community and our home became a sort of staging post for them on their way to and from the mission. On one occasion we were asked if they could hold their 'deanery' meeting at our home. The members of the Bethlehem community have remained good friends to this day.

Patrick had gained a PhD in Social Anthropology and, by the time we met him, had spent the better part of 25 years studying the Shona people, their language, culture, values and customs. Father Pat became a firm and dear friend of the family and spent the last decade of his life, when he had retired, living with us. Over the years, he helped us to understand the 'humanity' of the people who were our neighbours in the adjacent Tribal Trust Land[2] (TTL) and our Christian response to different peoples. But at this time, early in the 1970s, his knowledge of the language of the people and his awareness of how they appreciated those who took the trouble to learn the language persuaded Di and me to start chiShona lessons with him. On most farms in Rhodesia, the lingua franca was known as *chilapalapa* (in South Africa *fanakalo*), a degrading 'master and servant' language that did not allow for conversation or lead to any depth of understanding. Although we never became fluent in chiShona, the knowledge we had and the use we made of it helped tremendously in developing trust between us and the workers on the farm, and later in our work after independence. On the farm it meant that I could now greet my workers in their own language, which again led to improved relations and was to stand me in good stead when the liberation struggle finally reached the Belingwe farming area in the mid-1970s.

As our farm bordered the Belingwe Tribal Trust Land, our immediate southern neighbours were the multitude of people living there. And as my understanding of their needs grew, I was able to do such things as allowing their cattle to graze on the farm during drought periods and providing water for them. In winter they were able to cut thatching grass on the farm to repair their homes, and Di ran a small clinic and a sewing club for the wives of the workers. These neighbours provided seasonal labour when it was needed and we provided transport to hospital or the local clinic when necessary. In essence, life on the farm between 1968 and 1974 was idyllic, remote from the political turmoil and the escalating civil war. However, I had realised soon after I took over the farm that the wages of the farmworkers were totally inadequate and addressed this straight away, giving the more senior staff wages in accordance with their responsibilities.

This was something unheard of in many other farming areas, where some farmers did not even pay their workers, but allowed them to graze their own cattle on the farms instead. Our staff were incredibly grateful for this, but it did not make us particularly popular with some of the farmers in the area, an attitude that may have been strengthened when I began to push for agricultural workers' pensions shortly afterwards.

Moving to Belingwe also made us relatively close neighbours of Garfield and Grace Todd, whose Hokonui Ranch was about 30 miles away. Garfield had been Prime Minister of Southern Rhodesia – a progressive under whose guidance race relations had begun to improve. His own party, however, believed that he was moving too fast towards racial equality – white fears about shared schools, hospitals, cinemas and swimming pools,

..... Grace and Garfield Todd.

were vocally expressed. Accordingly they rejected him at a Party Congress in 1958, replacing him as Party Leader with Edgar Whitehead. After Ian Smith's illegal declaration of independence in 1965, he had become a major thorn in the side of the Smith government, and was consequently detained in his house and its immediate environs in 1965. My father had supported him politically and they had become firm friends. Our own friendship with the family stemmed from our meeting his daughter Judith when she was at the University of Rhodesia with Di's brothers, Peter and Patrick. Our physical closeness made it possible for us to visit the Todds when Garfield was detained on his farm, which was to cement our close friendship, and Garfield was responsible for guiding me towards the political action we later took.

Notes ··

1   Bona Mugabe, the mother of the President, was a humble and saintly
    woman who had been among the early Christian community formed in the
    Kutama Mission area. I met her several times while working in the Diocese
    of Chinhoyi. Despite her son's position, she continued to live in a simple,
    small house near the mission until she was no longer able to care for herself,
    whereupon she moved to her son's home in Harare.

2   The land that was set aside for black Rhodesians was known first as 'reserves'.
    Later, under the Land Tenure Act of the 1970s the land became Tribal Trust
    Land. After independence they became known as Communal Areas.

··

CHAPTER 4

Voices of Opposition

After UDI most of the senior black politicians were in detention and many others had left the country to avoid that fate, as well as to garner support for the nationalist movement in independent African countries. Those outside the country were also trying to establish external infrastructure for their parties and to nurture the embryonic guerrilla struggle for Rhodesia. One such politician was Herbert Chitepo, who left Rhodesia in 1962 and as early as 1966 began to organise military incursions into Rhodesia. However, within the detention camps much was happening and indeed the political struggle was being conducted from there. Consequently many whites were surprised and unprepared when the guerrilla war started in earnest in 1972.

In 1968 and 1969 Smith, having failed to negotiate an agreement with the Labour government in Britain, decided that new constitutional proposals should be formulated in an effort to secure the future for white Rhodesians, while assuring the black majority that their concerns were being taken into account. The resultant 1969 Constitution was as bad a Constitution as it is possible to get, but it reassured the whites and increased their devotion to Ian Smith. When Smith took the 1969 constitutional proposals to a referendum and white voters overwhelmingly accepted them, the black leaders reacted vehemently, denouncing them and once more stating that the door to negotiations had been slammed in their faces.

Smith had made efforts to reach some agreement with the British Labour Government through a couple of farcical meetings on board various British warships but to no avail. The Tories, however, having taken over from the Labour Party, sent the Foreign Secretary, Sir Alec Douglas-Home, to negotiate with Smith and, surprisingly, they came to an agreement that would be implemented if the majority accepted the terms of the agreement.[1] Lord Pearce was sent with a commission to test the opinion of the majority. This 'Test of Acceptance' was really the first time the views of the majority had been sought in any political process. As most of the prominent black politicians were still incarcerated, they persuaded Bishop Abel Muzorewa of the United Methodist Church to lead the black response and he did so with remarkable success, travelling up and down the country calling for a 'no' vote and the settlement proposals were rejected in no uncertain terms when the time came. By far the majority of whites accepted the proposals, but Garfield Todd and his daughter Judith courageously supported their rejection by the blacks by speaking strongly against the settlement. This led to their detention, to Judith's hunger strike and to her being manhandled and force-fed by the Rhodesian security police.

Bishop Muzorewa was then asked to lead those nationalists who were not in custody in a loose alliance that became the African National Council. Later he was to lead his own party, the United African National Council (UANC) into a settlement with the Smith government and much later became the first black Prime Minister in the country.

At about this time I began writing letters to the editors of national newspapers, mainly The *Bulawayo Chronicle*. I found a good deal of satisfaction in being able to have my political say, even if only through the letters column. The Rhodesian Front was an easy target because it made so many basic blunders and had some really strange bedfellows. At that time the daily papers in Salisbury (*The Rhodesia Herald*) and Bulawayo (*The Bulawayo Chronicle*) and the Sunday papers – the *Sunday Mail* in Salisbury and the *Sunday News* in Bulawayo – were unafraid to take the government to task despite the censorship that had been imposed at the time of UDI. Using the letters column was surprisingly effective. The letters seemed to be well read and there were many replies, mostly brickbats, but there were a few bouquets. It is quite surprising how many people read letters to the press and how the letters affect them. Many years later I was at a party in Sinoia. I was new in the town and so I knew very few people. I sat down next to a lady I had not met and introduced myself:

'Hi, I'm Mike Auret.'

A pause followed, a 'pregnant' pause, then:

'Are you M T H Auret?'

'Yes I am,' I replied.

'Well, I hate you,' she snapped.

'Oh, I'm sorry,' I said, laughing, 'but I don't think you know me.'

'I know you, alright,' she replied, 'you used to write those terrible letters to the press about Smithy and the RF!'

The Rhodesian Front (RF) government had imposed censorship on the day of UDI, giving it the power to exclude any news items it did not want the public to read or hear. This was the first time there had been any such censorship since the end of the Second World War. The editors responded by leaving large, blank spaces in their papers wherever an article had been censored. This practice was soon prohibited by law, but it had shown that the print media was determined not to be cowed by the cavalier actions of the government censorship board. The broadcast media, however, under the guidance of a South African propaganda expert, Harvey Ward, became the mouthpiece of the Rhodesian Front party and government. Using a five-minute programme after the main evening news, called Quirks and Quiddities, the Rhodesia Broadcasting Corporation (RBC) tried to belittle or berate any person who stood against the government or criticised its actions. There were many other propaganda programmes and the vernacular stations worked hard to convince the black majority that the Rhodesian Front government was looking after its best interests.

Early in the 1970s, although the liberation struggle had not yet started in earnest, the deteriorating political situation persuaded us to join the political fray. I had always had grave reservations about Smith and his party, but there was very little in the way of opposition to it. However, a new party called the Rhodesia Party was emerging. It had a strong leadership and we believed that the policies it espoused could lead to peace and stability and, ultimately, to democracy. The original leader of this party was a triumvirate of Allan Savory, an ecologist; Roy Ashburner, a farmer; and Dr Morris Hirsh. These three managed to draw together all the more liberal opponents of the RF and created the most effective opposition up till then. Di and I joined the party in its early stages and were part of the development of the grassroots of the party. At the first party congress in 1970, Allan Savory emerged as the leader of the party, and as the party grew in numbers and confidence, it brought new enthusiasm and hope to Rhodesian politics.

In 1972 the Rhodesia Party had its first test against the Rhodesian Front in a by-election at Hippo Valley in the lowveld where, although it lost the election, there was sufficient support and interest to make it worth continuing. The need to correct the political imbalances became even more urgent at the end of 1972, when guerrillas attacked Altena Farm in the north of Rhodesia. This attack signalled the beginning of the all-out guerrilla war that was to escalate in the years ahead.

After the lowveld by-election, the Rhodesia Party consolidated itself and Di and I spent much of our after-hours time visiting people, holding meetings and raising funds for the party and for the general election that would be called whenever Smith felt he had the best opportunity of retaining all 50 seats in Parliament. Smith had shown himself to be a past master at choosing election dates, announcing them when the opposition party was in disarray and at its most vulnerable. That opportunity came in July 1974; the Rhodesia Party was in disarray after a nasty and petty leadership squabble and was now under the new leadership of Tim Gibbs, the war was intensifying but was not yet at its height and, remarkably, the economy was relatively buoyant. So Smith grasped the opportunity to call an early election. Tim Gibbs' father, Sir Humphrey Gibbs, had been the last Governor of Southern Rhodesia and had shown extraordinary courage and determination after Smith had declared UDI by refusing to move out of Government House (Rhodesia's State House) and by maintaining contact with the British Government until Smith declared Rhodesia a republic.

.....Addressing supporters during the 1974 election.

I stood in the 1974 election as a candidate for the Bulawayo Districts constituency. Di and I took three weeks' leave and campaigned hard. We campaigned separately, but each with a partner, and walked incredible distances in our commitment to talk to each voter in our constituency. Di had some very frightening encounters with dogs – some of which were set on her by RF supporters – but in spite of all our efforts we could not shake the voters' confidence in Ian Smith and his government. The respective party policies were of no concern to the voters; they were happy with Smith and they would vote for him come what might. During my door-to-door canvassing the conversation would usually go something like this:

'Good evening, I'm Mike Auret, your candidate for the Rhodesia Party.'

'We're voting for Smith.'

'No sir/ma'am, Smith is standing, unopposed, in the Umzingwane constituency. This is the Bulawayo Districts constituency and you have your own MP.'

'Who is that?'

'Alec Moseley.'

'Never heard of him, I'm voting for Smith.'

Such exchanges – and there were many similar ones – were very depressing for me. However, although we lost in the Constituency (and in the country) a third of the voters in the constituency voted for me and

I saved my deposit. As non-racism was one of the core principles of the Rhodesia Party (RP), it was heartening that so many coloured and Asian constituents gave tremendous support to the election effort and even provided food for the helpers manning the polling stations, strengthening our belief in a multiracial future. The RP had not registered any black voters, as one of the provisions of the 1969 Constitution was to allocate separate seats for white and black Parliamentarians (with blacks representing for the most part constituencies in the rural areas): 16 seats in Parliament to black Rhodesians, of which eight would be popularly elected and eight appointed by the College of Chiefs. However, very few blacks registered to vote and even fewer exercised their vote. One successful Parliamentarian to be elected in a south-west constituency was Mr Lot Dewa, who won his seat by 152 votes. His constituency included the Belingwe Tribal area and we became friends and, later, 'comrades in danger'.

To our great disappointment the Rhodesian Front again won every seat and Rhodesia continued on the path to self-destruction. However, the experience brought us a greater understanding of the overall political situation and, perhaps more importantly, it showed us that the black people believed that our efforts to stand against the RF were worthwhile, and those with whom we had discussions viewed our efforts very positively. Even on the farm the workers had heard and read of my campaign and were pleased by the efforts we were making.

During the election campaign, I suffered a deep vein thrombosis and a pulmonary embolus and was quite ill by the end of it. I spent several weeks in hospital and then, while recovering on the farm, I started to read Alan Paton's prophetic book, *Cry, the Beloved Country*. Suddenly extraordinary feelings were stirred up within me and I found myself weeping uncontrollably whenever I looked at the book. A visit to the doctor confirmed that I was on the edge of a nervous breakdown and he recommended that I should exclude politics from my mind and take some leave. So we went off for a holiday to Coffee Bay in the Transkei, during which time I did little but sleep. The holiday seemed to rejuvenate my nervous system and I returned to the farm and to politics with renewed fervour.

Notes ···

1 Sir Alec Douglas-Home in 1964 defined the five principles under which
   independence could be granted to Southern Rhodesia. They were: (i)
   Unimpeded progress to majority rule; (ii) Guarantees against retrogressive
   amendments of the Constitution; (iii) Immediate improvement in the political
   status of Africans; (iv) Progress towards ending racial discrimination; and
   (v) British Government insistence that any proposal for independence be
   approved by the people of Rhodesia as a whole. Harold Wilson added another
   principle, namely: (vi) No independence before majority rule. (This last
   principle was excluded in the agreement between Douglas-Home and Smith
   that led to the 1971 Pearce Commission 'test of acceptability', which ended
   with the absolute rejection of the agreement by the African people.)

···

CHAPTER 5

The War Years

In the second half of 1974 John Vorster, the South African Prime Minister, together with Presidents Kaunda (Zambia), Nyerere (Tanzania), Machel (Mozambique) and Khama (Botswana), established the 'détente' exercise in the hope of finding agreement between the Smith government and the nationalist leaders to bring an end to the war. But to do this the nationalist leaders Joshua Nkomo, Robert Mugabe, Ndabaningi Sithole and others had to be released from detention. This happened in November 1974 in order to give them time to prepare for the conference, which was to be held at the Victoria Falls in August 1975. The list of delegates included many other prominent nationalists already outside the country, such as Herbert Chitepo and Josiah Tongogara, who was to become the commander of the

.....*With President Nyerere in Tanzania. The author is visible at the far right.*

ZANLA forces. The censorship regulations at the time made it unlawful to name any of the nationalists in the media, so it was difficult for whites at this time to either know of or follow the movements of such people, even if they were interested in doing so. Unhappily that conference ended after only a brief and farcical meeting on the Victoria Falls Bridge between Rhodesia and Zambia. After this the ANC led by Muzorewa broke apart into a number of nationalist parties.

In 1975, Mozambique achieved its independence. For Rhodesia that meant that there would be no more fuel coming in through the port of Beira, from where a pipeline had been built to bring fuel to the Feruka refinery near Umtali in the eastern part of the country. For a few years after UN sanctions had been applied against Rhodesia, Britain had sent ships to blockade Beira, in a vain attempt to prevent fuel supplies coming through. The ludicrous situation arose where the British Government was spending in the region of a million pounds a day on the Beira blockade, while a British petroleum company was supplying fuel to Rhodesia through South Africa. The independence of Mozambique was in fact a far more successful blockade, as the new government was determinedly 'anti' the Rhodesian government.

An independent Mozambique also meant, more seriously, that the military front now opened along the entire length of the eastern border. This brought our farming area into the war zone as it were, and it was not long before guerrilla and counter-guerrilla actions began there. Quite regularly security force groups would call at our house looking for somewhere to rest (on our lawn) or for something substantial to eat. As the war escalated, so too did the need for security forces, in both numbers and variety. Units such as the infamous Selous Scouts, the Police Anti-terrorist Unit (PATU) and the Grey Scouts (a mounted unit, both on horseback and in armoured cars) came into being and prosecuted the war vigorously. The following three years were filled with confusion, anger, disillusion and trepidation, but they were years, too, when my understanding of Christian principles grew and my sympathy for human suffering made me determined to maintain pressure on the Rhodesian Front government to change its destructive policy.

In 1975, the Justice and Peace Commission (JPC), established by the Rhodesian Catholic Bishops in 1972, published the first of three documents revealing the extent of human rights violations committed by the Rhodesian security forces against the civilian population. Entitled *The Man in the Middle*, it described the plight of ordinary rural people who were literally in the middle, between the security forces and liberation forces, generally called 'terrorists' by the white population. This was another area of confusion for me. There is absolutely no doubt at all that the forces of liberation used terror tactics in their campaign; they raided civilian homes, attacked women and children, committed barbaric acts against innocent people considered to be 'sell-outs', used landmines indiscriminately and murdered unprotected missionaries. But were not the tactics of the security forces as terrorising? Armed, camouflaged men were breaking down the doors of huts in which families slept, shouting all the time and arresting the men of the house; helicopter gunships fired incendiary bullets into the roofs of grass houses, terrorising the occupants, and thousands of civilians were killed in what was alleged afterwards to be 'crossfire'. Is this not terrorism? The difference that gradually became clear to me was that the Rhodesian security forces were supposed to be the forces of law and order; they should have upheld the laws and protected the rights of the people, but they did not. Instead they terrorised the people living in the TTLs, while alleging they were fighting 'terrorists'. So went my thoughts during these years.

I still had friends in the military, men with whom I had served, whom I had trained while an instructor at Llewellyn Barracks on the outskirts of Bulawayo and with whom I had formed good relationships, and I found it hard to believe that they would be involved in acts of brutality. If the JPC report was truthful, then 'our' forces were committing these atrocities; if the report was exaggerated or untrue, then my faith in the church was brought into question. I did not want to believe the JPC reports, but I knew some of its members, one of whom was my brother-in-law, Patrick Doherty, who at that time was the JPC Chairperson. I was to discover later that not only was the report true but it in fact revealed only the tip of the iceberg.

There were, of course, lighter moments in all of this. One occurred in the run-up to the 1974 election, when Reg Cowper, one of the junior ministers in the Rhodesian Front government, said at a public meeting that the number of military call-ups would be greatly reduced within a year. By 1975 he had become the Deputy Minister of Defence and it was now his duty to inform the country that it was necessary to 'increase the number of call-ups' due to the widening of the military front.

In the following year, 1975, the war arrived in our area in earnest. Military vehicles could be heard moving past our house, which was right alongside the main road to the Belingwe TTL. The military built a lookout post on the peak of Mount Belingwe, the highest point for miles around, which was also the northern boundary of the farm. All the farmers erected high fences, put up huge lights around vulnerable points and installed a radio that was in contact with the local police station at all times. We reported in each morning and evening and if anything untoward was happening.

It was while our fence was being erected that my workers approached me to tell me not to erect the fence; that if and when the *vakomana* (literally, 'the boys') came, the workers would ensure that I would not be attacked. I replied that if I did not have the fence many people, not least the police, would question the fact that I considered myself to be safe. They agreed then that I should do as all the other farmers in the area were doing, but assured me again and again that I had nothing to fear because of the relationship we had with the 'local' people. The 'security' offered by the fence was enhanced by an alarm system that, when triggered, would indicate which sector of the fence had been touched. I erected four huge lights that lit up most of the area surrounding the house, built walls to protect windows from rifle fire and put up grenade screens on all the windows. All these precautions were replicated around the district and indeed all around the country. The security of the farmers was of great importance to the government as they were indeed the first line of defence and abandoned farms were passages through which the guerrillas could operate.

However, the fence with its security alarm and the radio brought the entire family right into the centre of the war. The radio could be turned down, but could not be switched off entirely, so every incident in the area, whether an attack on a farmer's house, a landmine incident or a police/ military contact with the so-called terrorists was broadcast directly into the passageway which ran between our bedrooms. As most such incidents occurred at night it meant that our older children, when home from board-ing-school, and especially our youngest son, became increasingly afraid and unable to sleep. It was the fence and the alarm system, however, that was to trigger the greatest amount of anxiety and fear. Anything touching the fence, whether a leaf in the wind, an animal on the prowl, a cow in the field, or an armed attacker, would trigger the alarm. I can remember some very anxious nights in 1976. On one of these the alarm went off, again and again, in the space of a few minutes. Immediately I doused the huge lights and then, armed with a revolver and accompanied by my eldest son Peter who was armed with a shotgun, left the house and moved down to the sector of the fence indicated by the alarm. Pete was 13 at the time. From there we had to traverse that sector, moving as quietly as we could, and never knowing what was ahead of us. Meanwhile the rest of the family were on stand-by; all had specific tasks – Stephen stood ready to switch on the flood-lights at a shout from me and Margaret stayed close to the phone in case we needed assistance. Di always had the first-aid kit at the ready, at the same time holding our youngest son, Michael, to diminish his fear. We found nothing that night and in some ways this was worse. Our children showed enormous courage throughout this frightening time, but these ex-periences affected them deeply. Later in the same year, to maintain the confidence of the farmers, a group of older men were called up and sent to protect farmhouses, spouses and families both during the night and while the farmer was at work during the day. These good people were known as 'bright-lights' and initially we were glad to have their company. Later it became clear that we were part of their surveillance.

It was also during 1975 that I first met Robert Mugabe, although the name meant nothing to me at the time. I was attending a JPC meeting at the home of my brother-in-law Patrick Doherty, and met Mugabe, who was then a member of the ZANU Central Committee. He had just been released from detention in order to attend the talks arranged by John Vorster, the South African Prime Minister, which were to be held on the Victoria Falls bridge. However, I remember little of the man from that occasion.

Shortly afterwards, Mugabe took over the leadership of ZANU from Sithole and his name began to crop up more often in the overseas media. On the farm it came into the conversation of my workers quite regularly. There seemed to be a burgeoning of hope among the labour force and I was pleased that they did not exclude me from their discussions. Often the cattle dip at dipping time was their forum for politics and I was interested to discover how much they understood about what was going on and why. There is no doubt that this knowledge came largely from the clandestine meetings the *vakomana* held among the people at night. These meetings were known as *pfungwe* and they usually went on all night, leaving the gang not quite up to scratch the following day. My foreman, Magama Zinjiva, finally explained all this to me when I chastised him and the gang for their sloth. Zinjiva, over the years, had become a friend and colleague rather than simply an employee and he was to suffer for that friendship later in the war years.

This was the beginning of a most difficult time for my family and me. I was known to oppose the Rhodesian Front regime and we began to be treated with suspicion by the local police force. I found that my sympathies lay not with the security forces or the guerrillas, but rather, and with gathering strength, with the generality of the black population and, of course, my immediate neighbours in the TTL. The first example I had of the brutality used by the security forces in the area was when a young worker who had been with us a year or so – a likeable but cocky youngster – was on his way home one evening after work and he was stopped just outside the farm boundary by a group of soldiers in a vehicle. According to him, they questioned him about the 'terrorists' and he disclaimed any knowledge, whereupon a soldier pushed, or rather stabbed, a bayonet through his left foot, pinning it to the ground and holding him there while they beat him up. I knew nothing of this at the time but when he did not turn up for work for six weeks, I presumed that he had deserted. However, when he did return I called him in to explain his absence and he showed me the entry and exit wounds on his foot. He then told me the story and said that he had been kept at the Mataga hospital until the wound had healed. I believed him, knowing that war created situations in which people – normal, good and moral people; people that I knew – might do atrocious things, this being one of them. This was proven time and time again on all sides during the long and brutal war.

I was nevertheless outraged by the youngster's story and, leaving Di in the care of the 'bright-lights', I drove immediately to Gwelo, where I burst into the office of the Provincial Commissioner of Police – a man who knew me – and in great anger told him the story. He promised to check it and come back to me. To his credit, he did come back to me; he confirmed that the story was true and that steps had been taken to put a stop to that kind of interrogation. However, my trip to Gwelo and the response of the Provincial Commissioner clearly did not please the local policemen, as a quiet but determined kind of harassment started from that time.

Shortly after this incident, two men from the TTL came to see me to tell me of the systematic rape of young girls by the policemen at a camp in Mataga, a small township in the TTL. These policemen would go to a homestead and pick up young girls, telling the parents that they were to be employed to do domestic chores around the camp. After a couple of weeks these girls would be returned and more collected from another homestead. The girls complained to their parents about being used as 'wives' by the policemen. I took this case to a lawyer friend in Bulawayo, Ewan Greenfield, who prosecuted the case and those policemen were removed from the area.

In all, Ewan Greenfield took up four similar cases that we brought to him on behalf of people in the communal area south of the farm, and won all four. This did not endear us to either the police or the local farmers. Security Force activities began to increase in the area about this time, and Mnene Hospital, a Swedish Lutheran Mission Hospital, became a target for constant harassment by the security forces because the young black doctor there was treating wounded guerrillas, whom he saw simply as patients. One night, while treating such a patient, he was called to attend to another patient outside. As he left the building he was shot. A witness to the incident attributed the killing to the Selous Scouts[1] who were operating there. The Selous Scouts was a highly trained specialist unit, which was given the most secretive tasks and was well-known for its 'dirty tricks'. Soon after that incident word was brought to me by a trusted friend, Lot Dewa, the MP for the area, that the military had put out the word that they 'would get Dewa and Auret before the war was over'. Now the security fence around the house became a protection against attack from the Selous Scouts, and each day when I left to attend to the cattle on the farm, I locked Di, the children and the staff into the area bounded by the fence and took the key with me.

I was by now more torn than ever about my role as a Christian and the question of 'non-violence'. Both sides in this war were killing and using terror tactics (the people I had known in the army, my neighbours, the guerrillas who sought to 'free' the black people) and now for the first time I and the family were in danger of being subjected to these same tactics. How was I to react if faced with an aggressive attack on myself, perhaps at the dipping tank? How could I prevent the security forces from killing my staff? Could I protect my family without firing a weapon? These thoughts haunted me, but I was more than ever convinced that peace could be achieved only through dialogue between all the peoples of the country, black and white, including the nationalist leaders. The war brought home to me, above all, the futility of violence as a means of achieving peace. I determined from then on to do everything I could to protect my family, staff, and the local people (both black and white), in whatever way I could, using the press, the law and the Catholic Church to expose what was happening and to appeal for peace.

These feelings were really at odds with those of the generality of the white population, they were indeed a serious deviation from my own past. The growth of this new response, I believe, was the result of the new closeness to the faith I had reached through discussion with Pat Galvin and many other priests who practised and taught a rather radical doctrine. But confusion and conflict were ever present in my heart at that time, though conviction grew – so it was an extraordinarily difficult time. Another aid to this change was the ease with which Di and I related to our black neighbours and black people in general. They responded to us with great kindness and friendliness and so it was impossible to see them as the enemy. I believe that I probably owe my life and the lives of my family to the fact that our workers and our black neighbours protected us.

Over the following two years the police in Belingwe picked up several of my workers for questioning. On one occasion, foreman Magama Zinjiva and one of my drivers, Hlangano Moyo, were taken to the police station, and Moyo was seriously beaten up. Knowing how little they were fed at the police station, Di went in to see the staff and to take food to them. She arrived unnoticed by any office personnel at the station and saw Magama through the window of an office and went immediately to the window to talk to him. He was clearly disoriented, and started weeping when he saw her. He told her that they had put 'wires on his head' and had given him terrible shocks, and that afterwards he had signed a paper. Di left Magama in tears, and as she walked towards the car, she heard raucous laughter coming from a 'hippo' being washed by two young policemen. They found her reaction to a black man's pain hilarious. When Moyo returned to the farm the following day I took photographs of his badly swollen face. He told me that Zinjiva had been taken away from the station that day, possibly to the police post in Mataga, some 35 miles into the TTL. I immediately went to the District Commissioner (DC), Ian Bisset, explained what had happened and made a sworn statement which, with the film from my camera, was put into his safe. He then offered to take me to Mataga to find the foreman. The journey to Mataga was in his mine-proofed vehicle but was nonetheless nerve-wracking. When we arrived at the police post we went to see the officer-in-charge, who swore blind that Zinjiva was not there. He allowed us to look into the rooms of the station, and of course we did not find him.

Some days later Zinjiva returned to the farm. Before he would even speak to me he called the gang together and told them, with tears streaming down his cheeks, that he had been beaten and treated with electric shocks until he was unconscious. When he recovered, he was given the treatment again until he signed a statement saying that 'Marko had had contact with the *vakomana* and had indeed fed them'. He added, 'So if they come to pick up Marko (the name by which the local people knew me) it will be my fault.' Di and I were deeply moved by his courage in speaking to the workers and taking the blame for what he thought was his betrayal of us. He told us that the police were actually questioning him in Mataga when they saw the DC's vehicle arrive, and as we approached the front of the building he was pushed out of a window at the back and warned not to make any noise.

I was angry and unsure of what to do, so I phoned my father in Essexvale, where he had retired. His calm and clear thinking and his certainty that I was not 'guilty as charged' was what I needed, and he gave me some sound advice. A few years previously a policeman named 'Cordy' Hedge had been the member-in-charge in Belingwe and he and my father knew each other well; my father now advised me to go to Hedge, a very senior police-man by this time, and get his advice. I drove up to Salisbury, went to see Hedge and described to him what had taken place. He told me to leave it with him and he would ensure that the statement by Zinjiva was destroyed and that there was no question of prosecution. He must have taken some action as the harassment stopped for some time and things went back to normal on the farm – or as normal as the war situation would allow.

To digress a little, I had long been a follower of the remarkable Allan Savory,[2] an astute politician, a determined conservationist, a man who overcame childhood polio and who has achieved great things in the world of range management. At that time he was a consultant ecologist who was trying to promote a grazing system on large-scale cattle farms on which the land was deteriorating for lack of grazing management. I sought his expertise in an effort to improve the grazing management of the Belingwe farm. In the late sixties he had given me a basic short-duration grazing scheme, which I applied with very good results. In 1975 he came to the farm to upgrade my system to his new 'wagon-wheel' system. This meant that I needed to do a great deal more development on the farm to bring six 'wagon-wheels' into being. Many miles of fencing were required, with old fences to be realigned and four new dipping and treatment centres to be built, from which the fences would radiate. To assist me with this development I employed Theo Ferreira, a primary development officer in the government's Department of Internal Affairs who had a great deal of experience in building dipping facilities and who spoke chiShona fluently. He and his family moved onto the farm and over the following couple of years we created three 'wagon-wheels'.

Unfortunately, however, Theo was subject to the call-up for military service and, early in 1977, when he was away on call-up, and his family was fortunately off the farm, the guerrillas attacked his house (about eight miles from our home). The house was burnt to the ground and nothing remained of the furniture or personal effects. Theo's car, which had been parked in the workshop alongside the tractors, lorry and other farm implements, had been destroyed. I was astonished that no other farm equipment had been damaged in any way. But this was explained when I saw the notes that had been left for me by the guerrillas.

Not knowing that Ferreira's cook had come from Gatooma rather than the Belingwe area, the guerrillas gave him notes which were to be given to me. At first light the 'gang' had taken the tractor and trailer and driven to the main homestead to inform us of what had happened, and I had accordingly informed the police before heading for the other section. On my arrival at the burnt-out homestead the cook allowed me to read the notes, but was determined to tell the police of their existence and so I left them with him, and he accordingly gave them to the police on their arrival. These notes were addressed to 'Dear Marko' and said that I would notice that they had destroyed only the property of the soldier and had left all the other equipment and vehicles unscathed as they knew that I was a 'good man' and it was not their intention to harm me. The young policeman who had investigated the incident and taken the notes, called at our house on his way back to Belingwe to ensure that we knew that the notes would be given to his superior. For us it was an extremely worrying few hours, for although I was confident that the police had no evidence of my having had any contact with the guerrillas, the notes gave the impression that I was 'one of them'.

The member-in-charge called me to the Belingwe police station and showed me the notes. Their suspicions were obvious, but they were aware that I would take action against them if they considered any arrest, as I had done twice before about police behaviour with the local people. The local Farmers' Association was meeting that day at the home of my neighbour, John Hofmeyr, who had been ambushed recently, and I showed the members the photocopies of the notes. I assured them that I had not had any contact with the guerrillas and was not in any way supporting them. The farmers, my neighbours and friends of many years, appeared to accept my word and no action was ever taken against me. However, I am sure that there were farmers who were sceptical about my denial.

On the following day, however, two police vehicles, one of which was a mine-proofed 'hippo', drove on to the farm and took the main road to the other section and the 'destroyed house'. In their determination to get there quickly, the young policemen in the Land Rover overtook the hippo and four miles past our house hit a landmine. Fortunately no one was killed, but the vehicle was destroyed. A couple of days later another two vehicles drove onto the farm at 4.00 am, heading for the other section; en route one stopped at the main homestead and, without consulting me, had picked up one of my workers, Micah Zhou, to travel with them. On their return journey, needlessly using the same route, the vehicles were ambushed. The driver of the lead vehicle was killed, and Micah was shot in the thigh. His leg was amputated later at Shabani Hospital. The second vehicle made it through the ambush and the driver arrived at our house terribly shocked. After gulping down a cup of tea he was able to make contact with the base to report the incident.

That was the last incident on the farm, although incidents continued around the district and we continued to lose cattle. To get a break from the tension and anxiety, later that year 1977, Di and I went on an overseas holiday to Switzerland. In Switzerland we stayed with Father Pat Galvin at the Mission House in Immensee and visited the Swiss home of our employer, who instructed me to sell off all but a few head of cattle, to keep the farm on as tight a budget as possible and to grow no crops in the coming season. We thought this was simply a precaution to ensure that the farm did not lose too many cattle and that I did not have to spend too much time away from the house. But it was the precursor to the complete shutdown of the farm and the end of our employment there. Soon after Christmas he and his son came to tell us the news and, although I feared for the future of the farm if we were not there, I accepted the reasons he gave for closing down and started searching for alternative employment.

At about this time I received a phone call from John Deary, then the Chairperson of the Justice and Peace Commission (JPC). He told me that Brother Arthur Dupuis, the Organising Secretary of JPC and a Marist Brother, was due to retire and it had been suggested that I take on that position. I was stunned. Here was an unsolicited offer of employment when I needed it, but in an organisation despised by most whites in Rhodesia. Di and I prayed about it and I spoke to my father again. Initially, he was against my taking the post, as he was not convinced that the church had taken the correct stand on various issues; indeed, his attitude reflected that of most whites. After lengthy discussions, however, and with his understanding of what had happened to us on the farm, he accepted that it was a good opening for me. So I accepted the post. Leaving Belingwe was heartrending. My father had moved the family there in 1952, so for me it was a 25-year association with the place and the people. We were leaving our friends, our workers and a home we had loved. The Farmers' Association gave us a small party and presented us with a set of silver wine goblets. The workers held a bigger farewell gathering for us at which many tears were shed and the local chief spoke of the great affection in which the people held us. He thanked us for what we had done and ended his speech by saying, 'You are white people, but you have black hearts'.

Letting go of something I had loved was frightening for me, but the prospect of being able to serve the church and find a new direction, a new way to serve the people of the country helped me to overcome the fear and to look forward to this new life.

Notes

1 Allan Savory is an ecologist who spent many years in the Wildlife Department in Rhodesia. He was responsible for bringing the short-duration grazing system to the country and he was deeply concerned at the obvious deterioration of the land, both tribal and commercial. An abrasive politician, he served briefly as a Rhodesian Front parliamentarian and subsequently led the Rhodesia Party for a short time. He was forced to leave Rhodesia because of the policies of the government and he lived for some years in the United States. He has since returned to Zimbabwe where he runs an ecological training establishment.

2 The Selous Scouts was a secretive and infamous Rhodesian Army unit that made cross-border raids into Zambia and Mozambique, practised the 'turning' of guerrillas and subsequently employed them to search and report on the guerrilla situations. This unit was thought by many to have committed some of the atrocities for which the guerrillas were held responsible.

CHAPTER 6

The Catholic Connections

Starting work with the JPC in April 1978 was an extraordinary experience for me. Suddenly I was in a group of people who were all of like mind politically and, in most cases, religiously. I did not have to explain myself to them or justify my political stand; I was simply a part of them. I felt comfortable there, like putting on a favourite jacket; more comfortable than I had felt for years. Here in Justice and Peace, the question of whether or not this war, or any war for that matter, was a 'just war' and whether it was morally acceptable to fight on either side could be discussed. And I hoped and believed that through the commission I could contribute in some way to bringing about a lasting peace in the country.

My own confusion over this issue arose partly because for nine years I had attended a Catholic senior school, St George's College in Salisbury, and for the greater part of that time it had been my intention to become a priest. However, in my last year at school I fell in love with the lady who became, and still is, my wife. That put paid to my 'vocation', and I had no idea what career I would follow. Ultimately I joined the Federal Army and became an instructor. But when I look back it is incredible to me that a boy who had wanted to spend his life saving souls should now opt for a military life that was likely to involve killing people. And I had chosen this career without any censure from the priests I consulted. It is an historic fact that the church has been involved in the bearing of arms since the Crusades and that a number of Catholic schools maintain cadet corps where warfare is taught. At St George's College the cadet corps had a proud record; it was the only Rhodesian school to have been awarded Regimental Colours for the contribution made by St George's old boys in the two World Wars. Later our three boys were to attend Downside School, a prestigious Catholic school in Somerset in Britain and there too there was a cadet corps teaching methods of war. The confusion in my mind over the morality of bearing arms continues to this day, although as the years went on I became more and more convinced by the words of Pope Paul VI at the UN in 1966 that 'war is evil', and to my mind all alternatives must be explored before so tragic a step is taken.

Brother Arthur Dupuis, the Organising Secretary, remained in the office for several weeks to help me find my way and learn who was who, and to introduce me to the Bishops and to the staff of the Bishops' Conference. The Bishops' Conference and three of its commissions – Education, Social Development, and Justice and Peace – were housed in two charming old colonial-style houses on the corner of Fourth Street and Selous Avenue in Salisbury, with polished wooden floors, embossed steel ceilings, a quaint ball-and-claw bath and a real chain to pull in the toilet. There were 20 or so members of the commission at that time, most of them serving voluntarily and working very hard in their own time to carry out the work of the commission. We met every Wednesday evening to plan the action for the coming week, to decide what we should or should not tell the Bishops, to analyse what had happened or just to share our thoughts. Part of the work of the commission was research into a host of relevant areas, in a series that reflected the forthcoming change from Rhodesia to Zimbabwe covering topics such as the land question, education and health. Preparing sermon suggestions for the parish priests was also a JPC task. As the commission was extremely unpopular among white Catholics, the clergy often found themselves dealing with a backlash. But writing the sermon notes was also an effort to propagate the Social Teaching of the church[1] that had been the central theme of the Second Vatican Council, and which contained so much that was relevant to the situation in the third world generally and to our situation in particular.

In my first week I attended the Annual General Meeting of the Bishops'

Conference, and began to understand where each of the Bishops stood with regard to the political situation and the role of the church in it. There were six dioceses in Rhodesia: Harare, an archdiocese; Bulawayo, later to become an archdiocese; Umtali, the see of the inimitable Bishop Donal Lamont; Wankie; Gwelo; and the Prefecture Apostolic of Sinoia, later to be elevated to diocese status. The Prefect Apostolic of Sinoia, Monsignor Helmut Reckter SJ, was also the President of JPC at that time. Bishop Lamont had been the previous President and had been by far the most outspoken of the Bishops on issues of justice and politics. He had been arrested by the police for instructing his priests not to divulge any information about the *vakomana,* as that would surely and seriously endanger them. He was tried in the High Court where he made a very significant speech from the dock that was later published and caused great anger and indeed consternation in the government. Bishop Lamont was found guilty and sentenced to a term in prison. But before he was required to serve the term he was deported and continued 'the struggle' from his home in Ireland. He subsequently returned to Zimbabwe after independence to hand over the Diocese of Mutare to the new bishop, Alexio Muchabaiwa.

The Catholic Church had established itself very early in the colonial history of the country and had developed many missions with schools and/or hospitals, bringing learning and healing to many people. It also established the first schools for whites, the Dominican Convents for girls and St George's College for boys. It was in the mission schools that most of the nationalist politicians, including Mugabe, were educated and Catholicism remains the most widespread of the mainstream denominations in the country. Church and state had enjoyed cordial relations until the middle of the century, partly because the Prime Minister and Archbishop Aston Chichester SJ were good friends. In 1960, however, the church began ruffling feathers in Rhodesia. Having been the first to introduce multi-racial schooling that year and having made a plea for peace at the time of UDI, it now took the government to task over the 1968 constitutional proposals and thereafter it was to maintain a high profile on the Rhodesian political scene.

In March 1972 the Bishops' Conference set up the Catholic Commission for Justice and Peace – more commonly called the Justice and Peace Commission (JPC). Its tasks initially were to learn and teach the Social Teaching of the church as it related to human rights and development; to investigate specific violations of rights; to report to the Bishops; and to take appropriate action, with the guidance of the Bishops, to correct such violations. Almost from the start, however, the commission began to see its role primarily as the defence of human rights, in response to Pope Paul VI's call in 1969: 'If you want peace work for justice.' It was not long therefore before tensions developed between the commission and the Bishops' Conference, with the JPC wanting to steam ahead with its work and the Conference trying to slow things down to allow time for reflection. It was at this point that I joined JPC.

There was also great tension between the JPC and the country's white lay Catholics, as the majority of them supported Smith and approved of the war effort. They were upset that a Catholic organisation should be so unpatriotic as to criticise the activities of the security forces and many of them refused to believe that 'our boys in the bush' could commit the atrocities the JPC was claiming. One group of lay Catholics based in Borrowdale, a suburb of Salisbury, was convinced that the commission members were inspired by communism and were therefore enemies of the church.

This tension worried me considerably and so, after a couple of months in office, I set off around the country to address as many of our parishes as possible, explaining to them why the JPC was taking this stand on human rights violations.[2] The journey was quite successful. Many of the people who attended the meetings claimed to have understood better by the end of a meeting. However, they still did not like what we were doing. Others were not quite so polite – at a meeting in Shabani (later Zvishavane), while I was speaking a car started hooting right outside the window of the hall – every minute or so a loud blast. This was quite distracting for all of us, so the parish priest went out to see what was happening. He came back to report that one of his parishioners who disapproved of JPC wanted to declare his disapproval loudly; he would not do so personally as he did not want to be seen at such a 'traitorous' meeting. The hooting continued for a few minutes, but finally the car drove away. Perhaps he felt he had made his point.

After another meeting in Bulawayo, I went to the Bishop's house, and later that evening there was a knock at the door and a tall, gangling black priest came into the room and introduced himself. I did not catch his name, but we sat and talked for a couple of hours. He clearly supported the work of the commission and I felt a strong liking for him. At the end of the conversation I said, 'Sorry, Father, I didn't catch your name?' 'I am Pius Ncube,' he said. This was the man that I had been warned about before starting my trip. I was advised by one of my colleagues to be careful should I meet Pius Ncube as he was a racist. But neither then, nor at any other time since, have I observed any racist feelings in this good man. Pius Ncube later became Archbishop of Bulawayo and a courageous advocate for human rights, justice and democracy against Mugabe's excesses.

Those first months in JPC convinced me that I had found my niche in life. I was at last learning about the Social Teaching and using it as I

.....With Archbishop Pius Ncube of Bulawayo, a man of extraordinary courage.

understood it should be used. I was also beginning to understand the politics of the church, its structures and operations.

I was sure that what I was doing was valuable to the Church and the country. Through the JPC analysis of the occurrences taking place daily and our commentary on them, the JPC intended to inform the consciences of Catholics especially, in the hope that influence could be brought to bear on the government to bring about a negotiated end to the war and the enormous suffering of the people.

Notes

1. In 1959 Pope John XXIII inaugurated the Second Vatican Council, which was to produce The Social Teaching of the Catholic Church, which sought to bring that Church into the 20th Century and prepare it for the 21st.
2. Since independence many books have vindicated the stand JPC took and have proven the truth of its reports. Perhaps the most recent of these is *Scribbling the Cat*, by Alexandra Fuller (Pan Macmillan 2004).

CHAPTER 7

The Last Throes of the 'Colony'

In 1978 the JPC had just completed an analysis of the Salisbury Agreement[1] of 3 March 1978, signed after Ian Smith had brought together three internal leaders, Ndabaningi Sithole, who had recently been replaced by Mugabe as the ZANU leader; Bishop Abel Muzorewa, who had excelled himself in leading the opposition to the Smith/Home agreement; and Chief Jeremiah Chirau, whom Smith presented as a genuine, indigenous leader of the black majority. The agreement was to lead to the first majority rule election, before which the country would be governed by an interim government made up of four prime ministers and two ministers, one white and one black for each ministry, to prepare the way for majority rule. The people of the country were assured after the agreement was signed that the war would wind down and peace and stability would eventually return. The agreement also promised a referendum on the ending of racial discrimination, after which there would be no further need for war.

The Salisbury Agreement, however, was doomed to failure because it excluded the two most important leaders, Nkomo and Mugabe, as was pointed out by the JPC analysis. The Bishops, however, decided against publishing the JPC document until some minor amendments had been made, and until they felt the time was right. When the analysis was published in July 1978, the war had escalated considerably and the situation was exacerbated by the fact that the three black prime ministers had recruited armies of their own. These became known as 'auxiliary forces' and they increased the suffering of ordinary people enormously.

1978 and 1979 saw the final push by the Rhodesian Front government to hold back the tide of African nationalism, but it was clear that the military was not coping. The nationalist forces now controlled large tracts of country, acts of sabotage were being carried out even in Salisbury, where the vital fuel depots were destroyed by rockets and two bombs were placed in shopping areas; travelling became nightmarish, with escorted convoys being the only way to be relatively safe; both the effects of sanctions and the cooling of the South African response brought the country almost to crisis point.

They were also years in which great atrocities were committed on all sides. In Domboshawa, just outside Salisbury, security forces shot 27 civilians, ostensibly 'in crossfire'. In Gutu 102 civilians died, shot while attending a meeting called by the guerrillas, again caught in 'crossfire' when security forces tried to kill the men holding the meeting. A civilian passenger aircraft was shot down en route from Kariba by ZIPRA forces and, to make the crime doubly atrocious, nine of the survivors were butchered by the same forces less than an hour after the crash. Some weeks later a second aircraft was brought down by ZIPRA; this time there were no survivors. At Elim Mission in the east of the country all the missionaries and their families – men, women and children – were butchered by ZANLA forces. Bishop Adolph Schmitt, a priest and a religious sister were murdered near Lupane, where five months earlier a German doctor, Johanna Decker, and a religious sister had been taken from St Luke's Hospital, beaten and murdered. Three Jesuit priests and four Dominican sisters were also killed at Musami Mission near Salisbury. While it was claimed that the killing of Bishop Schmitt and his party and the atrocity at Musami mission were carried out by guerrilla forces this was never proven and to this day the identity of the killers is a matter for conjecture. The Rhodesian Front government deported Bishop Donal Lamont, several priests and religious sisters for 'subversive activities'. Two priests, Ignatious Mhonda and Patrick Mutume (later Bishop Mutume) were arrested and tortured in the Mutare Diocese and several other religious workers were deported, generally having been accused of 'assisting the terrorists'. There were many religious lay men and women who taught at schools and treated patients in hospitals in rural areas, regardless of who they were, and later continued to do so despite the dangers of the war. They often paid the ultimate price for their faith and Christian love with their lives. Among those who continued to run Outreach clinics throughout the war were Srs Patricia Walsh and Gaudiosa Dippert in the remote Chilimanzi TTL. There were of course many other heroes of that time, who remain unsung.

The Rhodesian security forces also committed atrocities in neighbouring countries, during these two years. Both Zambia and Mozambique suffered devastating raids by the Selous Scouts, ostensibly to clear 'terrorist' bases in those countries. In Zambia the base was quite close to the capital, but in Mozambique the relevant areas, Chimoio and Nyadzonya, were quite remote. Many people were killed or injured in these raids. The government asserted vehemently that the bases were indeed 'terrorist' bases, but the nationalists were as vehement in their claims that they were refugee camps. In reality there was truth in both claims and the nationalists were guilty of using refugees to shield their military bases, but the speed and violence of the raids and the very high death toll in the camps surely indicate an enormous overkill.

They were indeed terrible years, but all through the war there had been atrocities, and there was a great sadness now in the country, with so many people going off to war, so many dying and so many losing parents, children and siblings on all sides. Many marriages broke down and many women were violated and above all most people went to bed hungry every night. Operation Turkey, put in place by the security forces to keep food away from the 'terrorists', also kept it away from the people who needed it most. The government had set up so-called 'protected villages' throughout the country, removing hundreds of thousands of people from their homes and confining them to very small fenced areas, which they could leave only during the day, and then only if there were no disturbances in the area. I gave a talk in the Anglican Cathedral hall in Salisbury on the effects of malnutrition on the young caused by 'Operation Turkey' and when the talk and the questions were over we trooped outside to find a senior Catholic layman waiting for us, who shouted, 'You communists, you bloody communists!' This was, sadly, not an isolated incident.

The failure of the Salisbury Agreement either to end the war or reduce the effects of the isolation of the country meant that a political solution was unlikely. These years saw the experiment of the 'interim' government, the removal by law of racial discrimination, the election of the first black government and, finally, the Lancaster House conference.

Notes

1   The Salisbury Agreement reached between the Smith Government and three selected black politicians, Bishop Abel Muzorewa of the United Methodist Church, The Rev Ndabaningi Sithole (one of the founding leaders of ZANU and subsequently the leader of a party he called ZANU (Ndonga), and Chief Jeremiah Chirau, a malleable tribal leader. Briefly the agreement offered a 100 seat Parliament, of which 72 seats would be held by blacks and 28 seats would be reserved for whites. Of the white seats 20 would be elected by whites on a separate roll and eight would be elected on the general role, but in the first election the eight would be nominated by the Rhodesian Front Party.

CHAPTER 8

Church and Politics

The great suffering and the lack of progress towards peace persuaded the JPC to ask the Bishops' Conference to send a delegation to all the political leaders to describe the suffering to them and to encourage them to work more emphatically towards a settlement. Thus, a delegation representing the Bishops' Conference and the commission was sent to Lusaka to meet the nationalist leaders, Mugabe and Nkomo.

Arranging the meetings was extremely difficult and frustrating, as it required special flight arrangements by private aircraft to fly from Rhodesia to Malawi. To fly to Malawi from Rhodesia in those days meant that the pilot had to issue a flight plan stating that the flight originated in Messina in South Africa rather than Salisbury, as President Banda had a working relationship with the government of South Africa, but would not have any dealings with Rhodesia. From Malawi we flew with Zambian Airways to Lusaka. The political arrangements were no less difficult. They were made through Josiah Chinamano, the Vice-President of ZAPU who was still able to travel within Rhodesia, and through a variety of contacts for ZANU.

I was in my office on the day before our departure when Chinamano came in to tell me that the trip would have to be postponed as something more important had come up. He would not enlighten me and I really could not think of anything that was more important than our task. I argued with him for some minutes and then he said, 'Well, phone Mr Nkomo.' He gave me the number in Lusaka. I dialled, got through and spoke to the man himself. I was amazed. We were at war with ZAPU and here I was talking to its leader on the phone without interruption from those listening to our calls, as had happened before. After brief opening pleasantries, I explained the problem to him and Nkomo simply said that we should come anyway and that he would make the necessary alterations to previously planned meetings. I was very relieved, not only because it had been quite difficult putting the trip together, but also because the Archbishop of Salisbury had not been too enthusiastic about the undertaking and I did not want him to call it off. This was the first time I had spoken to Nkomo and I was pleasantly surprised by his kindness and decisiveness.

We arrived in Lusaka on a Sunday evening and were accommodated at Luisha House, the home of the local Jesuits. On the following morning we met Joshua Nkomo. To describe him as a large man would be to understate the case – he was enormous, both figuratively and literally. He had great presence but a gentle charm and I liked him immediately. Later, he and some of his senior party officials, including George Silundika, who subsequently became the Foreign Minister in the first Zimbabwean Government, took us to State House where we met President Kaunda and attended the arranged meetings.

At the meeting with Nkomo, Archbishop Chakaipa of Salisbury read, haltingly, a two-page introduction in English for our discussions that I had prepared. It spoke in depth of the suffering of all the people of Rhodesia. At one point in the discussions that followed we told Nkomo that his forces had been responsible for the murders of two Jesuit missionaries at St Rupert's Mission in Makonde. With some vehemence Nkomo denied that his forces would have committed these crimes. He placed the blame on the infamous Selous Scouts, but we had irrefutable evidence that ZIPRA had been the perpetrators. I mention this because his reaction was in marked contrast to Mugabe's when told of atrocities committed by his soldiers.

That first meeting with Nkomo, on the Monday afternoon, was well under way when suddenly Kaunda himself interrupted it to call Nkomo out of the meeting. We did not see Nkomo again until the Wednesday. The meeting proceeded with the ZAPU officials and arrangements were made to show us the refugee camps, including the camp for unmarried mothers, and the training being given to many of them in Zambia. The disappearance of Nkomo from our first meeting remained puzzling until much later, after we had returned to Salisbury, where we learnt the explanation, and it was bizarre! *Time* magazine printed a photograph of Ian Smith outside State House in Lusaka with the story of his attempt to persuade Nkomo to join the Internal Settlement proposed by the Salisbury Agreement. Suddenly it became clear that Kaunda had taken Nkomo away from our meeting to meet Ian Smith in a separate room in the same house. It seemed incredible. Smith had been in the same building at the same time as us, without either party being aware of it. I believe that had Smith known of our presence he would have tried to squeeze some propaganda value from it when he returned to Rhodesia, but we heard nothing at all from the government about the trip.

On the following day Brigadier Garba, the Nigerian leader, arrived in his private jet, and when Mugabe arrived in Lusaka the Brigadier immediately whisked him off to Nigeria in order – we learnt later – to explain to him why Nkomo had met with Smith without him, although the two of them were joint leaders of the tenuous Patriotic Front. The Patriotic Front had been formed on the advice of the 'Front Line' presidents, as sympathetic nations were tired of dealing with two external nationalist forces. While the Patriotic Front was never a strong joining of the two parties, it did serve its purpose, particularly at Lancaster House later. The two armies, however, never found any common ground and whenever they came in contact with each other, violence ensued.

Whatever Garba said to Mugabe, it obviously did not please him, for when we met him on the Saturday he was clearly still very angry. Our meeting with Mugabe was more satisfactory than that with Nkomo. Several of the senior ZANU people attended the meeting, including Edgar Tekere, Josiah Tongogara, Fred Shava and Simon Muzenda. Josiah Tongogara was Commander-in-Chief of the ZANLA forces.[1] When introduced to me he said, 'Auret? Belingwe? Yes, when my people go into the south-east of our country, they already know your name.'

Again, the Archbishop read the introductory document slowly and hesitantly in English. While he was reading, I remember feeling irritated that Mugabe seemed not to be paying attention. He fiddled with his glasses – a characteristic he never lost – looked out of the windows and generally appeared to be distracted. However, when the Archbishop came to the end of the paper, Mugabe spoke to each point made, almost chronologically – clearly, a remarkable intellect. He was far more open and truthful than Nkomo had been. He acknowledged that his forces had committed atrocities, as had the security forces, the so-called forces of law and order in Rhodesia. But he reminded us that his lines of communication were from Maputo to Karoi, some 3 000 miles, and that it was extremely difficult to maintain discipline over that distance. He promised, however, that if we knew of such incidents and reported them to him as they occurred, he would ensure that disciplinary action was taken against the offenders. Whether or not that ever happened I do not know, but his openness in discussing these things impressed me tremendously. After our meeting I was left with an enduring feeling that I had met the future leader of the country and that he was worthy and capable of undertaking the task.

Unfortunately, however, these meetings did not appear to have any effect on the war or the suffering, and so in March 1979 I was sent with two senior clerics, Bishop Tobias Chiginya of Gwelo and Monsignor Helmut Reckter SJ of Sinoia, to meet the new Pope, HH John Paul ll. To our amusement the Cardinal who met us at the door greeted me with the words: 'Why are you not dressed correctly, my Lord?' He was under the impression that I too was a Bishop – as was the Vatican newspaper report of that visit. We were to ask Pope John Paul II to use his influence on the world leaders to bring some conclusion to the war. He granted us an audience of 30 minutes and in that time discussed the report that I had written for him previously on the situation in Rhodesia. I was amazed at how quickly he responded to our request. Early the following week we met officials in the West German Foreign Affairs department who assured us that the Pope had already been in touch with the Ambassador in Rome and other western ambassadors.

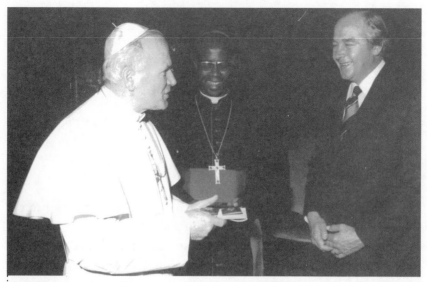

.....*Visit to HH Pope John Paul II, March 1979, with Bishop Chiginya (centre).*

I cannot say whether or not the Pope's action helped, but it is a fact that at the end of that year the Lancaster House talks took place and the peace agreement was signed. Being in the Vatican and meeting Pope John Paul II were moving experiences for me, as he was a man of great intellect and great compassion.

Notes

1   Edgar Tekere was the Secretary General of ZANU (PF), but was dismissed from the party after making strong accusations against it. He later formed his own party, the Zimbabwe Unity Movement, and was probably the first to accuse the government of rigging the elections; Josiah Tongogara, was the charismatic and well-liked commander of the ZANLA forces, and died in questionable circumstances almost on the eve of independence; Fred Shava was a party functionary who became the Minister of Social Welfare and who resigned after being named in the 'Willowgate' scandal; Simon Muzenda was the long-time second-in-command of ZANU and later the Vice-President of Zimbabwe.

CHAPTER 9

Exiled in England

Towards the end of 1978 the Chairperson of the JPC, John Deary, Brother (later Father) Fidelis Mukonori, a Jesuit, and I had been to America to meet the American Justice and Peace Commission and selected politicians, again to describe the current situation truthfully to America. There had been undercurrents of pressure from certain quarters in that country to remove sanctions on specific Rhodesian products, notably chrome. It is perhaps interesting to note here that Rhodesia, 'the last bastion of western democracy', was selling its chrome to the Soviet (communist) bloc, which was, in turn, selling it on to the United States, which bought it gratefully despite the Cold War. Economics are stronger than political morality! While we were on that journey, John Deary's house was subjected to a grenade attack. While his wife Pat was asleep in the bedroom a grenade was thrown in through the window; by the grace of God she was not injured, but several pieces of shrapnel went directly into John's pillow and had he been there he would certainly have been seriously injured, or may even have been killed. The attack was glibly ascribed to 'terrorists' by the government and the media, but little investigation was carried out.

For some months now I had been subject to abusive language, in phone calls made to our home and, on occasion, from irate white passers-by while we walked in the streets. In addition we found our mail was being intercepted and opened, and our telephone was being tapped (clearly on the instructions of the Rhodesian Government). One day while Di was on the phone to a friend, the call was interrupted by a loud clicking noise, and then she heard her own voice and last few minutes of conversation, being played back to her. Needless to say she added some very strong words to the tape, for the benefit of the technician. Di was particularly fearful that the children might answer the phone and hear what the callers thought of their father. Of greater importance, however, was to say nothing on the phone or on paper that could be used by the Smith regime against me or the JPC. However, worse was to follow.

While I was in Rome, Di had received my call-up papers. I could imagine her anxiety, as I had received a similar military call-up the previous year, which I had refused, and we had waited anxiously to be informed of the military's reaction. We were fearful as the months went by and we heard nothing, and learnt only some time later that the Army actually did not know what to do with me – they did not want me, as an Officer with previous experience in Intelligence, to have access to sensitive information. This call-up was very different, however, as it included, on the one form, a summons to report for two call-ups with a two-week break between the two and clearly stated 'that failure to report for duty within seven days, was punishable with a prison sentence'. This was probably in preparation for the elections in April. Clearly my trip to Rome and the time I had spent in the Rhodesia Party, the only opposition to Smith, as well as the efforts I had made to obtain justice for the victims of the Rhodesian security forces and my work with the JPC had angered the authorities.

Di immediately contacted one of the priests with whom we were friendly and he took the form to discuss it further with the Bishops. Their immediate response was that I should not return to Rhodesia, as I would most certainly be jailed, and in jail I could not serve the JPC and would most probably be ill-treated. They therefore recommended to me that I remain outside Rhodesia. In the next few days it was also decided that Di and the family should leave as quickly and quietly as possible to avoid any attempt to hold her to ensure my return. A very traumatic few days followed, as few people could be told and so much had to be left to the courageous few to deal with after Di had left – none more courageous than our housekeeper, Smellina Moyo, who had come with us from the farm and had been with the family for 12 years. She met the Military Police at our front door on the seventh day, the day I should have reported. She refused to let them into the house and kept insisting that we were not there.

The family was initially cared for by the Bethlehem Missionary Fathers at their Mother House in Immensee in Switzerland, while I went to England to find a job. When the family arrived in June we were accommodated and cared for with great generosity by Ian Linden, Director of the Catholic Institute for International Relations, and his wife Jane at their home in Bath. In July, however, we were settled in Kilmersdon, just outside Bath, and I was working in London. At that time Ewan Greenfield was also working in London, and his wife Pat found employment for me with a shipping and forwarding company with whom she did business. While working in London, I lived with Chris and Maggie Power during the week and returned home for the weekends. He was the Chairperson of the Racial Justice Commission and we met when we were both giving talks at a Justice and Peace meeting in London. Knowing that I was looking for accommodation I could afford, he phoned a few days later to ask whether I would like to have a room in their newly acquired 'too large' house. I was overjoyed and we struck a bargain – I got a home and, in the fullness of time, they got a baby-sitter.

The house in Kilmersdon belonged to Raymond, Lord Hylton, one of the few Catholics in the House of Lords. We had met after I gave a talk at the retreat centre Ammerdown, which was attached to his home, in May 1979. Lord Oxford had been the Chairperson at the talk and he had been less than polite about what I had had to say, as he believed that Bishop Muzorewa had legitimately won the April election and that he was therefore the legitimate prime minister of what was then called Zimbabwe/ Rhodesia. Lord Oxford had not understood the importance to the people of the two external leaders, Nkomo and Mugabe. However, Lord Hylton had been impressed by what I had had to say and that led him to offer us a house while we were living with the Lindens.

Lord Hylton also had a great interest in what was happening in Northern Ireland at the time, and particularly concerned with their search for peace. As that had for many years also been an interest of mine, he invited me to a meeting he had arranged with a number of people from various Northern Ireland political parties, to learn more about the issues and to discuss possible peace initiatives. The meeting, in church surroundings and with several church people attending, fortified my conviction that the church had a role to play in politics wherever there were disputes, particularly violent ones. During that time in England I gave several talks on justice and peace at various venues, which brought me into contact with many like-minded people whose convictions strengthened mine.

I was also asked to give talks on the Rhodesian situation at a number of functions, and I surprised even myself with the deep conviction I felt that finally, when democratic elections were held, Mugabe would emerge as the winner. We were in England during the Lancaster House talks, hanging on every shred of news we could glean from friends and the news media, and we celebrated with great joy both the electoral victory and the day of independence at Africa House in London with many hundreds of other new Zimbabweans, both black and white. The joy in Africa House that evening reminded me of the great joy that greeted the end of the war in Europe. It was palpable and contagious and the celebrations continued well into the next day.

The Early Mugabe Years

PART TWO

CHAPTER 10

Euphoria of Early Independence

As soon as independence had been declared Di and I wrote to Mugabe to offer our services in whatever field we could be of service. He replied personally quite soon afterwards, telling us that we were welcome to come back to the country and that we should submit our CVs to various government ministries. We were encouraged by this response and determined to do so. Accordingly I made arrangements for my return and Di followed later. The President of the JPC, Monsignor Helmut Reckter SJ, however, had already made other plans for me, both within his own diocese and within the commission. At that time the thousands of people who had been herded into 'protected villages' during the last phases of the war now wanted desperately to get back to their villages to till their lands and grow food, and this became the first urgent task for the diocese through the Catholic Development Commission. I was determined to do whatever I could to help redress the wrongs of the past, and so it was with great gusto that Di and I joined the drive for development by working in the Catholic Development Commission in the diocese of Chinhoyi (previously Sinoia). We also felt that this work was critical to bringing about the reconciliation proclaimed by the Prime Minister and to rebuild what had been destroyed by the war.

It was to the great credit of Mugabe's government that it immediately began the process of righting the wrongs of the past and, unlike any other newly independent country in Africa, began to implement development programmes where they were most needed – in the rural areas, particularly in the most remote areas, where every effort was made to ensure that education and health were more readily accessible to all the people. This was made possible by the remarkable response of Western donors, who, despite the new socialist policies, answered the country's calls for financial assistance very generously with both grants and loans to the government, thus ensuring that the development of the new social infrastructure went ahead apace with the political changes.

Di was the Chinhoyi Diocesan Development Co-ordinator, while I held the post of Agricultural Co-ordinator for the 362 agricultural groups being resettled in their villages. Initially, apart from agriculture, our work included the rehabilitation of health facilities, schools and dipping tanks and, later, the construction of refugee camps as people began to move into the country from Mozambique. For example, two mission hospitals in the diocese had been partially destroyed during the war, as well as a training school and several primary schools – they all needed rebuilding and refurbishing. This became Di's responsibility in the Diocese of Chinhoyi, which covered 65 000 square kilometres in the north/north-west of the country. Both the rehabilitation and development programmes were funded by Catholic agencies, such as Misereor, Cebemo (now Cordaid), Trocaire, Cafod, and Caritas.

To motivate the rural people to work alongside us to rehabilitate facilities, we used Mugabe's name unashamedly in urging farmers, and indeed other workers in the developmental field, to greater efforts. This was not always helped by the Political Commissars, however, who were carrying out political education on the ground. On one occasion, some youth living in the area near Marymount Mission hospital in the north-east, arrested a builder who had been working on an extension to the hospital, and took him to the Political Commissar. They alleged that on the previous evening, while drinking, he had used derogatory language while discussing Mugabe. When Di arrived at the building site, where no work was in progress, she was told about the arrest, and that the builder was being questioned at a nearby store. She drove immediately to the store and saw the builder chained to a tree, being chastised by a large group of youth and the political educator. Di immediately got out of the car, walked up to the builder and untied him, shouting all the time about what Mugabe would have to say about 'work stoppages'. The youths looked bemused and chastened – perhaps the speed of the action threw them off balance – but nothing further was heard of the incident and no further incidents of a similar nature occurred.

During the early months of 1980, the JPC (now renamed the Catholic Commission for Justice and Peace in Zimbabwe (CCJP)) was in the process of re-evaluating its task in the light of the new situation that seemed to hold such great possibilities for peace, for the upholding of human rights and for the development of a new economic order that would bring some prosperity to the people. I was elected Chairperson of the CCJP on my return, and combined this with my work in Chinhoyi Diocese. Most members of the commission felt that the church should move closer to the government, but when the Bishops' Conference decided to maintain some distance between it and the government, commission members at an acrimonious meeting in Gweru (Gwelo), asked the Bishops to separate the commission from the Bishops' Conference and allow it to work independently. The Bishops refused – correctly I believe – but this refusal led to the resignation of most of the members who had given such courageous and selfless service to the organisation and the country during the dark years of the war. I remained Chairperson of CCJP and set about rebuilding it, while carrying out my agricultural development work in the Chinhoyi Diocese.

On 2 February 1982 the CCJP held its Annual General Meeting in Gweru, with Prime Minister Mugabe as our guest of honour. The theme of the meeting was 'Socialism and the Social Teaching'. Perhaps I should explain here that the CCJP was tasked with, among other things, learning, teaching and applying the Social Teaching of the Catholic Church, particularly as it relates to human rights and development. We had asked him to address us for two reasons; first, we wanted to know his attitude to the commission and the work it would continue to do despite the new situation and, secondly, to discover how he viewed the Catholic Social Teaching. Mugabe was a Catholic. His upbringing had included an education from the Jesuits at Kutama Mission; he had been married in a Catholic Church in Ghana; had chosen the Catholic Archbishop to bless the new flag and had attended Mass in the Catholic Cathedral in Harare on the day after the independence celebrations; his government had set a path of reconciliation and development in which the church joined wholeheartedly. But he was an avowed Marxist – how could all this be reconciled?

At the AGM, after sharing lunch with us, Mugabe congratulated the commission on the work it had done to protect human rights during the former regime and encouraged us to continue with this work. He spoke about the socialism he espoused and called on the church to understand that his socialism was very similar to the Catholic Social Teaching. Indeed, he called on the church to give socialism a Christian face, with these words:

> If Christianity's main criticism of socialism or communism is that it is too much of materialism and very little of God, my retort is: Give it a God, the God of socialism, but please never the God of capitalism. In my view, true Christians should feel more at home in a socialist environment than in a capitalist one.

He spoke of his vision of reconciliation and development for all the people. There were no recriminations and no harping on the past, only a determination to ensure that the people be allowed to develop to their full potential. Everything he said impressed me tremendously. A Dominican sister, Sister Hyacinth Gerbecks OP, a specialist in the Social Teaching of the church, spoke after Mugabe and I was struck by the similarities between the two discourses. This meeting contributed greatly to my understanding of the church's Social Teaching and of the Christianity of the man I had come to admire so much. As he spoke I experienced a growing respect for him, for his intellect and his humanity. I was impressed by his sincerity and by what seemed to be an obvious respect for the church. By that time also it was clear that his government had every intention of developing the areas and the people so neglected in the past. Already hospitals, clinics and schools were being built throughout the country, particularly in the peripheral areas where the need was greatest. It seemed clear that Mugabe was committed to a brand of socialism that was to benefit the poor and did not contradict the Catholic Social Teaching.

At this time Di and I believed that this man shared our dream of a multiracial, egalitarian society, where the contribution of women would be recognised and where development would create an increase in the wealth of all the people. We somehow believed that his call for reconciliation was not simply pragmatic and that he would be happy to have the contribution of those white Zimbabweans who had chosen to remain in the country. We believed in him.

On the second anniversary of independence in 1982, it was with a great deal of pleasure that we accepted an invitation to the celebratory banquet at the Harare Sheraton Hotel. I can't say that I was impressed with the food that night, but I was impressed by the fact that Mugabe made a point of moving around among the guests during the meal, generally acting as a concerned host and saying a few words to each one he met. He also spoke to us for a few minutes, discussing our work as though he was really interested in it. This was only the second time I had met him face to face since he had come to power.

My admiration for him grew with each contact and in the months ahead I found myself putting him on a pedestal – a position from which I found it most difficult to displace him in the years that followed, despite everything that happened. It is perhaps understandable, therefore, that when the troubles in Matabeleland began in the same year, I found it easier to blame anyone but him for what was happening there.

CHAPTER 11

Worrying Trends

In the first two years of independence the country had transformed rapidly from war to peace, from fear of the future to an increasing sense of security for black and white alike, despite two major acts of sabotage, one at Nkomo Barracks armoury and one on the air force base in Gweru. Life quickly settled back into familiar but more secure patterns for whites and into hopeful new patterns for blacks. These early years of peace were rewarded by wonderful rainy seasons; they were years full of hope and the reputation of Robert Mugabe grew considerably.

It soon became clear, however, that the development needed throughout the country would require a substantial increase in the civil service and in government expenditure. Unfortunately, the economy of the country was not growing at the rate required to keep up with the social development, which led to more government borrowing. At the same time, Mugabe's insistence on continuing his Marxist/socialist rhetoric did nothing to encourage external investment in the country, investment desperately needed to develop employment possibilities and a more solid economic basis for the new nation. That rhetoric should have warned us that Mugabe was a determined socialist, with Marxist principles, and that his determination would not allow any deviation from his socialist aims.

The exercise of integrating the three armies, the soldiers of the former Rhodesian army and those of the ZIPRA and ZANLA liberation forces was under way, and the National Army quickly grew to about 70 000 – far too large and costly for so small a country. However, the exercise was important in placating the returning soldiers, reassuring them that they would have some share of the spoils. The integration exercise was not an easy one. The two liberation armies had never been at ease with one another, and the initial attempts at integration led to two violent upheavals in 1981 at Entumbane, the holding camp for both groups. The two armies were divided ethnically and politically, with the majority of ZANLA being chiShona-speaking and most members of ZIPRA speaking siNdebele. Historical rivalries and more recent political divisions had not encouraged the development of easy relationships between the two groups. However, the violence was finally brought under control and the integration exercise continued, though not before there had been a number of desertions from the new National Army, mainly of ZIPRA personnel, who believed that they would be disadvantaged by the greater ZANLA contingent in the army. It is probable that these deserters took their weapons with them and may have been among the 'dissidents' in the later turmoil. The violence at Entumbane led to the establishment of two commissions of inquiry led by Mr Justice Enoch Dumbutshena, later the Chief Justice, but the results of these investigations were never made public.

The incidents at Entumbane should have made me aware that the tension between these two ethnic groups was much more serious and volatile than the tension between the racial groups themselves. Indeed, the policy of reconciliation being espoused by the government had already succeeded in reducing the levels of racism quite substantially. At least on the surface and in public places, relations between black and white improved dramatically, despite the fact that in private many whites continued to harbour their racial and class prejudices, and many younger blacks started to harbour negative racial feelings themselves. However, at the time, the Entumbane incidents seemed nothing more than teething troubles in the new nation rather than the precursors of the more serious strife to follow.

During 1982 political tensions between the two nationalist parties, which were synonymous with the two ethnic groups, increased with ZANU (PF) accusing PF (ZAPU) of a variety of political and terrorist actions that arose from a series of violent armed robberies and murders occurring around the country. Somehow, the actions in the rest of the country were underplayed and called banditry, but those that took place in Matabeleland were publicised more widely. Many young people returning to the country after serving in the guerrilla armies, having had no education and finding no employment, simply took up their arms again in order to make a living from banditry. However, the acts of banditry that took place in Matabeleland soon became known as 'dissent' and the bandits as 'dissidents', a name that Mugabe was to use throughout the subsequent violence.

It was also clear that South Africa, then still in the grip of the Apartheid system, could not afford to have a stable, non-racial peaceful country on its borders, as that would give the lie to the white South African contention that blacks were not able to govern a country. It therefore set about destabilising Zimbabwe, using covert military and economic attacks. However, ZANU (PF) was always paranoid about enemies; the party seemed to need someone to blame for any of its shortcomings. At the outset South Africa was a clear enemy, then the 'dissidents' in Matabeleland, followed by RENAMO[1] the Mozambique resistance movement and, much later, the whites and the opposition parties. This was probably the reason the government clung to some of the security legislation brought in by the Smith regime and used it to terrible effect in the Matabeleland conflict and against six airmen who were charged with sabotage, when several aircraft were destroyed by explosives one night at the airbase in Gweru. It was commonly believed that this sabotage was committed by South African agents. These unfortunate men, before any hearing was held, were arrested and detained under this 'security legislation' for many weeks, and were severely tortured. When the case was heard in court, the torture they had been subjected to resulted in a 'not guilty' verdict (which was the correct one in any case).

The military wing of ZANU (PF) completed its training in 1982 and arrived on the Zimbabwean scene as the Fifth Brigade, led by Perence Shiri, who later became the Air Marshal commanding the Zimbabwe Air Force, a promotion that was a deliberate slight to the many people who had suffered at his hands. Although this unit was not part of the National Army, it was paid from the national coffers and it did the work for which it was designed – to do the party bidding with absolute loyalty, no questions asked. The headdress of the unit was a distinctive red beret.

Instructors from North Korea were brought into Zimbabwe to train the Fifth Brigade. It later emerged that these instructors were not particularly expert at military training but were adept at the methods of politicisation that they taught the recruits. At the 'passing out' parade of this unit it was given the name *Gukurahundi*, a chiShona word meaning the 'first rains which wash away the chaff'. (In Africa, when the women thresh and winnow the crops, the wind blows the chaff onto the ground; when the first rains come the chaff is washed away.) The Commanding Officer went further that day, tasking the soldiers with 'weeding out the dissidents'. But it was not until early in the following year, when the unit was deployed in Matabeleland, that we understood fully the implications of its name and purpose.

During the year stories began to circulate about the Central Intelligence Organisation (CIO), infamous in Rhodesia, using torture again on suspected 'enemies of the state'. At the CCJP we were concerned that the government's reconciliation policy meant that former members of the Rhodesian CIO and police were still employed in the same positions as they had been prior to independence, meaning that the technology of torture and some of the torturers had simply been transferred to the new nation. The stories were shown to be true when one of the former Rhodesian Front MPs, Wally Stuttaford, now an elderly man, brought a case to the High Court against the Minister of State Security and he was awarded substantial damages for having been subjected to brutal torture. After this case, the government reintroduced the iniquitous Indemnity and Compensation Act, retrospective to the date when Parliament had repealed the law.

The Rhodesian Front government had first promulgated this law in 1975 in order to protect ministers, the police force and other service personnel from prosecution for violations of human rights committed 'in good faith in the fight against terrorism'. The Zimbabwe government repealed the law in 1981 after a senior member of the ruling party had been acquitted of the murder of a farmer in the Norton area, using this law as his defence. The CCJP had congratulated the government on the removal of this legislation and so were understandably distressed at its subsequent reintroduction in 1982. As the CCJP Chairperson at the time, I issued a statement criticising this action. It was the first critical statement the commission had made since 1980 and it caused the Director to resign in protest.

Early in 1982 a cache of weapons was discovered on farms owned by PF (ZAPU). It should be remembered that arms and ammunition had been hidden all over the country during the war and during the repatriation of the guerrilla forces. It is also possible that the CIO deliberately buried these arms on the farms in order to increase the tensions between the two major parties. Dumiso Dabengwa, the ZAPU intelligence chief during the war and later the Minister of Home Affairs, was convinced that this was indeed the case and he linked it to the destabilisation efforts of the Apartheid government of South Africa. As a result of this 'discovery' and an abortive and particularly inept attack on the Prime Minister's residence, a curfew was imposed on Matabeleland, with arrests and detentions of PF (ZAPU) officials following.

The government sent troops and police into the high-density suburbs of Bulawayo, ostensibly to search for weapons. Reports reaching the CCJP indicated that this was simply a cover for extreme harassment. The political tensions between the two major parties continued to grow, both in and out of Parliament, but as ZANU (PF) had formed the government and had been so magnanimous as to include members of the minority party in a government of national unity and reconciliation, it appeared to stand on the moral high ground. This image of the party and the careful control on what was reported in the media enhanced the misconception in the minds of the population outside of Matabeleland that the government was carrying out its duty to protect the security of its citizens.

The deteriorating situation in Matabeleland and the reintroduction of the Indemnity and Compensation Act led to my next meeting with the Prime Minister. Bishop Patrick Mutume, the auxiliary Bishop of Mutare and Bishops' Conference-appointed head of the CCJP, and I, as the Chairperson, met Mugabe in his Munhumatapa office on 5 November 1982. He was aware of the purpose of our visit and he met us graciously and without any appearance of disquiet. Having first congratulated him on the remarkable development taking place in the country (this process of congratulations preceding any criticism became the norm over the years, as politicians demanded that the good be acknowledged, as if that would offset the criticism) the Bishop and I handed him a document explaining our concerns over the reports of torture, the reintroduction of the Indemnity and Compensation Act, the harassment of people in Bulawayo and our deep concern over the formation of the Fifth Brigade as the military wing of ZANU (PF).

We spoke at some length of these concerns and Mugabe heard us out patiently and without any apparent irritation. Indeed, in his reply he said that he was grateful for the report and for the fact that the commission was continuing to carry out its human rights 'watchdog' role. He claimed that PF (ZAPU) had been discovered in an attempt to take over the government by violent means and for his party to feel secure it was vital that there was a force which was absolutely loyal to the ruling party. Therefore it was necessary to form a military wing of the party. He spoke of the Fifth Brigade in such matter-of-fact terms that it was impossible for us to perceive any deceit, or indeed anything sinister in what he had said. He explained the torture and harassment as being 'simple over-enthusiasm' and lack of experience of the new 'policemen'.

In explaining the reintroduction of the Indemnity and Compensation Act, he selected his words carefully. He insisted that, while it was true that Stuttaford had been tortured, it was also true that the same Stuttaford had been a party to the signing of the illegal Unilateral Declaration of Independence in November 1965, and so it was impossible for him, Mugabe, to justify to his people the paying of the damages award made in favour of Stuttaford. Therefore, the law had to be reinstated and made retroactive. However, he assured us that it would be repealed at the appropriate time.

Our visit was reported in the press and the situation in Bulawayo did improve slightly for a while. This encouraged me to think that his intentions were not to allow his forces to violate the rights of his people. Once again, at this meeting I had felt a deep respect for Mugabe. I felt honoured to be in his office. I wanted to hear what he had to say; I wanted him not to be at fault; I hoped that I was doing him a service by bringing this information to him. As always, he spoke in measured tones and was neither glib nor dismissive. However, while his explanations were given with apparent sincerity, on this occasion I found that I was uncomfortable with them. This was for me the first indication of his ability to excuse any wrongdoing by his government or party, and this pattern was to repeat itself increasingly in the future.

Notes

1   RENAMO was a terrorist organisation created by the Rhodesian Government to destabilise Mozambique and to occupy the Mozambican armed forces to prevent them from coming into conflict with Rhodesian security forces that were operating against ZANLA forces based in Mozambique.

CHAPTER 12

Terror in Matabeleland

In the dying days of 1982 a passenger train came under armed attack near Bulawayo and nine people were killed. The attack was ascribed to 'dissidents'. On 26 January 1983, the Fifth Brigade was deployed in Matabeleland North to deal with this 'dissident menace'. I was based in Chinhoyi at the time, where I was the Bishop's secretary as well as being the CCJP Chairperson and I was completely unaware of the situation unfolding in Matabeleland. Chinhoyi is in the Mashonaland West province, quite distant from Matabeleland, and there had been no media reports from there except for claims of Fifth Brigade successes in controlling the dissidents. The first I heard of the troubles was via a phone call from the Chairperson of the Bulawayo branch of the CCJP[1], Joel Simon Silonda, a towering Matabele of great presence and moral courage. He asked me to come to Bulawayo because the Fifth Brigade had killed many people in its first onslaught in the North of the province and had perpetrated great violence against many others.

I thought at first that Silonda was exaggerating the seriousness of the situation, but felt sufficiently concerned to visit Bulawayo to see for myself. Having had a briefing from Bishop Henry Karlen CMM (now Archbishop Emeritus) who was deeply disturbed by the conflict, and several of the mission priests, I visited St Luke's Hospital in Lupane, where I spoke to Dr Davies, a woman of extraordinary courage who had served the people of that region throughout the liberation war and was now in the midst of great violence once more. She showed us some of the terrible wounds on the patients being treated and I was able to speak to several victims of the Fifth Brigade. I was deeply moved by what I saw and it was only then that I began to understand the extent of the violence that had been unleashed on the people of that region. I interviewed and photographed one man whose arms had been tied together very tightly at wrist and elbow with electric wire while he was beaten. He was left like that for some hours and now had lost the use of his hands. Nyamanhlovu is the area within the Matabeleland North Province where the Fifth Brigade began its onslaught. Another example of the violence of the first onslaught was the fact that just three days after the deployment of the Fifth Brigade, the soldiers rounded up a large number of men from the area of Pelandaba, tortured them, then shot them. Other reports coming through to CCJP included the fact that village members, who had not been killed or abducted, were frequently forced to watch others close to them dying slowly from injuries sustained from beatings, burnings, shooting or bayonetting. Villagers were warned not to seek medical help, and risked being shot for curfew-breaking if they did seek help. They also suffered massive material loss in the initial onslaught, losing homes and granaries. These were patterns that the military followed over the next several years.

On the drive back to Chinhoyi after this visit, I was very troubled; the horror of what I had seen at the hospital, the facts I had been told by the Bishop, by Silonda and others, and my growing anger at Fifth Brigade, the commanders and the North Korean trainers – all conflicted with my regard for Mugabe. I was confused but determined to ensure that Mugabe was informed about all that was happening, and that I would use the media also to try to halt the excesses of the military. At that early stage it did not occur to me that this was an all-out attempt to rid the country of the opposition political party, or even the vengeance of the Shona against their old enemy. I still believed that the military were combating dissidents, albeit with extraordinary and unnecessary violence against the civilian population.

However, before we had any idea of the enormity of the onslaught, I sent Dorita Field, then the Director of the CCJP, a most courageous woman from Northern Ireland, to complete my investigations and to prepare a report for the Bishops' Conference. This report, the first of four we were to make to the Prime Minister during this period, told of the detention and torture of many civilians, the indiscriminate killing of many more and the terror that was already becoming the life of the people of that region. It noted that the curfew imposed in 1982 was making it very difficult for the people to grow or obtain food. Matabeleland is drought prone and food is sometimes very scarce. The people there are pastoralists to whom livestock has always meant wealth, but their herds had been decimated by a combination of poor management, drought and confiscation by Rhodesian government forces from people considered to be assisting the liberation forces. Now, with their wealth so drastically reduced, they were forced to rely on crops for their survival. The crops failed in 1983 and the curfew made it impossible to purchase food. Once again, hunger was being used as a weapon of war. This report was completed and sent to the Bishops' Conference, where it was decided to send a delegation to the Prime Minister to ensure that he was made aware of the truth.

We presented the report to the Prime Minister on 16 March 1983, just six weeks after the deployment of the Fifth Brigade in Matabeleland. He had already received a similar report from a group of external NGOs; it had made him extremely angry at what he described as 'interference in the internal affairs of this new nation'. Therefore, it was with some trepidation that we decided to take our report to him.

With me at the meeting with Mugabe were Bishops Karlen, Reckter and Mutume, while Mugabe was accompanied by his Ministers of State Security, Mnangagwa and Defence, Sekaramai. Although they greeted us with the usual courtesy of the African people, the atmosphere was less cordial than at previous meetings. I felt this was due to the presence of the ministers, whom I believed were more aware than Mugabe of the true state of affairs in Matabeleland. They sat silent and grim-faced throughout the meeting. Mugabe heard our concerns and as we were talking he paged through our report. I thought that I had read in his eyes that he believed, perhaps for the first time, that something very serious was happening in

Matabeleland. In retrospect, however, I now believe that he was realising that we, the church representatives, had discovered the truth of what he was doing and that he knew that the church could become a problem he would have to face at some time in the future.

As the meeting drew to a close, Mugabe assured us that the intention of government was simply to rid the country of dissidents who were plotting to overthrow his government, with the help of South Africa and former Rhodesian forces. He promised to look into our concerns (this was reminiscent of Ian Smith's reaction to concerns expressed by the church), but said he was not convinced that the rights of innocent civilians were being violated in any way. The Bishops advised him that the Conference intended to publish a pastoral letter on the situation, and he made no objection. When, however, the strongly worded pastoral, entitled *Reconciliation is Still Possible*, was published on Easter Sunday that year, he reacted angrily, referring to the Bishops as 'pontificating prelates'. This reaction was the first intimation of the difficult relationship that would develop between the government and the church whenever the issue of human rights violations was raised.

Perhaps I should explain here that previously, when Mugabe had been taxed with the fact that some of his ministers were making outrageous statements on various issues at political rallies, he had retorted, 'When a politician is speaking at a political rally, he is speaking for the people, for effect, and not too much attention should be paid to what he says. If you wish to know what is really happening, go to see him in his office, when he will answer as a minister of government.' So when Mugabe railed against the Bishops' Conference, he was speaking publicly and I saw this speech as simply 'political'.

After this report there was a respite for the people of the region, when the curfew was lifted and military activity seemed to slow down. However, it was a very brief respite and then murderous actions continued. CCJP therefore began preparing a new report for the Bishops. The evidence gathered by me, other members of CCJP, Bishop Karlen, several of his priests and others, formed the basis of our reports to the Prime Minister.

The gathering of this evidence over several years was at times a terrifying experience. On several occasions I had to drive through North and South Matabeleland in a small Datsun motor car, knowing that the dissidents might be in the area, or worse, that I might be stopped by the Fifth Brigade. On one occasion when I had returned to Bulawayo from Brunapeg Mission in Mphoens, I heard to my great sadness of the murder of Andy McDonald and his wife at the gate of their farm on the same road I had used to return. Andy was a well-known and loved former Rhodesian and Springbok rugby player, with whom I had played many games of rugby while he was doing his military service in the late 1950s. He was a gentle giant who, while living in Zambia, had once been attacked by a lion, which he then had killed with his bare hands. He had come to live in Matabeleland after that experience. On another occasion I drove through Matabeleland North to visit Regina Mundi Mission, where the Fifth Brigade had killed several villagers and buried them in a mass grave on the mission land. This trip was all the more frightening as the roads in that area are composed of deep sand and my car had great difficulty moving through it. These times were distressing also as I had to interview many people who had suffered dreadful torture for no reason at all, or people whose family members had been murdered or had simply disappeared and who had no idea why or if they would ever be seen again. Many were not.

Much later, Nick Ndebele also had frightening experiences in the search for evidence. He had been arrested by the police near Lupane and thrown into the police cells, where he met several other detainees who assured him that his days were numbered, as no one left those cells alive. Fortunately he was saved when a religious sister, who knew he had gone there, arrived at the police station and told them she was looking for him and could they help. The presence of a church person caused them to release him. He did much courageous work in the area at that time.

In July 1983 the Bishops and I presented another report to the Prime Minister once again meeting in his office. This meeting was not at all cordial and our report was listened to in stony silence. However, he had obviously thought out a means to assuage our concerns and he promptly promised to set up a committee of inquiry to investigate our claims that massive human rights violations were taking place and to report publicly its findings. Once again, the relevant ministers were in attendance, as well as his army commander, General Solomon Mujuru. They made no contribution to the discussion, but the tension in the room was tangible and I felt uneasy for the first time in Mugabe's presence.

During these times I also spoke to foreign journalists occasionally about the situation as I was aware that publicity overseas about the violence would help to curtail it. It was not until August 1983, after a reminder from the CCJP, that the committee of inquiry was established under the chairmanship of a senior legal practitioner, Mr Simplicius Chihambakwe. The other committee members were retired Brigadier Mike Shute, who had been involved in quelling the Entumbane disturbances, a lawyer, Mr P Machaya, and a secretary, John Ngara, who was undoubtedly a member of the CIO. The committee was tasked with investigating the allegations of human rights violations in the areas affected by dissidents.

The committee began its hearings in Bulawayo in January 1984 and the CCJP gave our evidence in March. We had spent many hours recording statements from victims, making sworn affidavits, collating the evidence and gathering suitable witnesses. But before bringing witnesses to give evidence, we insisted that the Minister of Justice provide letters assuring the witnesses that they would not be prosecuted or harassed after giving their testimony. The committee set aside a paltry four days to take evidence in Bulawayo, but it was so overwhelmed by the numbers of victims wishing to tell their story that it was forced to return the following month to continue the process.

One of the witnesses we had brought was a young man who had been among about 25 others taken by Fifth Brigade to the banks of a dry river, near a school in Matabeleland North. These men had been lined up on the bank and shot; all of them fell, but to make sure they were all dead the soldiers moved among them and again shot anyone who seemed to be still alive. By extraordinary good fortune two survived, our witness and an older man, both of whom were wounded, but escaped the final shooting. Our witness, after a long, frightening and painful journey, had reached a rural hospital where his left arm was amputated. He gave his evidence clearly and dramatically and although Ngara tried to shake his story he was unable to do so. I was struck by the courage of the young man and angered by the callousness with which the secretary of the committee questioned him. Another part of the evidence we presented was a skull and several bones I had removed from a mass grave. The skull showed clearly that the victim had died from a gunshot wound in the temple.

This grave was among those found by the Anglican Bishop of Matabeleland, Bishop Robert Mercer, on the farm adjoining Cyrene, an Anglican Mission. The other occupants of that grave, and two other graves nearby, were young Ndebele men who had been removed from buses travelling on that road, taken behind a small hill adjacent to the road, accused of being dissidents and summarily shot at close range. There were at least three bodies visible in each grave; the soldiers had piled firewood on top of the graves and burnt the bodies before covering them with soil.

Visiting the site of these mass graves left me with a very heavy heart. I was deeply saddened by the wanton killing of these young men and I was appalled by the unfeeling way in which the dead had been buried and burned in an attempt to hide the crimes. This summary burial, repeated all over Matabeleland, was an affront to the culture of the people, to one of their most important religious rites. I was angry and determined that some evidence of these atrocities would be presented to the Chihambakwe Committee, so I took with me the evidence of the bodies we had found. Surely the committee's report of this evidence would persuade Mugabe to call off the Fifth Brigade?

This report, which must have included the three previous CCJP reports we had presented to the Prime Minister, was never made public despite the assurances we had been given by Mugabe in the July meeting. By now, however, Mugabe must have been aware that the CCJP had compiled much of the evidence and that I had been deeply involved in collating the data.[2]

Despite what I now knew about the Matabeleland tragedy, my regard for Mugabe was not diminished. I was content to lay the blame for the atrocities on the ministers, the military commanders, the soldiers themselves, but not the Prime Minister. I was convinced that, for the first time in Africa, a new leader was truly concerned for the plight of his people and determined to do all he could to improve their situation.

But looking back, it is clear that something had changed in Mugabe's perception of the CCJP and me in the mid-1980s. The meetings between him and the commission during the Matabeleland troubles were to be the last face-to-face business meetings I had with him. The commission was required on many future occasions to warn government of the effects of steps the party was taking, and on many occasions I unsuccessfully sought interviews with him to inform him, prior to informing the public, of a particular situation being created. It was our practice to send any statement or report we were producing to the Prime Minister first so that he could not say that we did not keep him informed.

Meanwhile, the government, working closely with the churches and the NGOs, was spearheading development in the rural areas. Schools, clinics, dams and dipping tanks were being built everywhere – except in Matabeleland. The people in the rural areas spent much time moulding and burning bricks for the new buildings. They entered into the new spirit of self-development that was engaging the country.[3] Di and I were involved in this sort of development work in the Chinhoyi Diocese and well knew of the tremendous changes taking place there, which mirrored those in other parts of the country.

But I was also still battling with the knowledge that, having read the commission's reports, Mugabe knew about the atrocities taking place in Matabeleland, and must surely be discomfited at my awareness of his failure to act. Yet when we met at a social occasion in November 1983 he behaved as though nothing marred our relationship. He had been invited to present the prizes at Chinhoyi High School, where our second son, Stephen, spent his final school year. He presented Stephen with the 'Sportsperson of the Year' award, smiling as he said, 'You're a chip off the old block.' During the lunch that followed he signalled across the room to Di and me, and invited us to sit with him. He was most friendly and chatted freely with us on various development issues. I came away feeling, again, a great respect and fondness for the man, in spite of my doubts and confusion over Matabeleland.

Notes

1   The Catholic Church in Zimbabwe at this time had six dioceses and each had a CCJP committee with its own structure. The National Commission co-ordinated the activities of the Diocesan Committees. I was then the National Chairperson.

2   The Chihambakwe report is currently the subject of a court action to force government to release it to the public and I believe now that Mugabe had already understood at that time that the report of the Chihambakwe committee would be very damning evidence against him if he should ever stand trial in the future. What happened during *Gukurahundi* is the subject of the report *Breaking the Silence: Building True Peace*, about which more will be said later.

3   So impressive was the development that some years later the CCJP commissioned Di to write a book on it; entitled *A Decade of Development*, it was published in 1992. It was written not only to record the development that had taken place in the country by the people themselves, in particular the women, but also to acknowledge Mugabe's encouragement of this development through his economic policies, wrong as they were in terms of global economics.

CHAPTER 13

A Flawed Democracy

The first post-independence election was due to be held in 1985 and more or less the same parties that had fought the 1980 election were lined up against one another again. ZANU (PF), PF (ZAPU), a very diminished UANC and ZANU (Ndonga) were attempting to represent the majority while the Conservative Alliance of Zimbabwe (CAZ), the Rhodesian Front under a new name, stood for the whites.

Early in the year it had again become necessary for the CCJP to issue a warning that if the violence did not stop the election could not be considered free and fair. There had been incidents of terrible violence in the Gokwe and Silobela areas, both of them contact areas between the two parties. Several people had been killed, homes and granaries burned and gangs of ZANU (PF) youths were marauding around in these contact areas causing great hardship. In Mashonaland also, the homes of some of the few remaining supporters of Bishop Muzorewa's UANC were destroyed and the people beaten up. However, the warning appeared to have been heeded as the violence diminished considerably.

The 20 seats reserved for whites through the Lancaster House agreement were again to be contested by whites only. The Conservative Alliance of Zimbabwe, which was later to be led by another Smith, Gerald, remained the only party, although several of Smith's erstwhile colleagues in the RF stood as independents. Unfortunately the majority white voters once again voted for Smith and his henchmen, who won 15 seats and the independents five. This result angered Mugabe greatly, as he had clearly expected that his magnanimity in pursuing a policy of reconciliation, and giving the whites three Ministers: David Smith in Finance, Dennis Norman in Agriculture and Christian Anderson in one of the justice ministries, would have ensured that the whites would respond by bringing more conciliatory people into Parliament. They did not. He railed against 'these racists' and in Shona threatened to 'kill those snakes among us'. I also was saddened by the white result but without any party to challenge Smith it was inevitable. Di and I simply did not vote on the white roll.

But Mugabe was far more angered by the fact that the people of Matabeleland voted almost entirely for PF (ZAPU), which retained the 15 seats in Matabeleland. I have no doubt that at this stage he thought that the people had been sufficiently cowed to ensure a change of loyalty – but he had seriously underestimated the Ndebele people, their courage and their loyalty.

So the results enraged Mugabe. In his address to the nation after the results were announced, he called once more for 'the weeding out of the dissidents' on national television. Almost immediately there were serious outbreaks of violence in many centres, notably Harare and Kwe Kwe. A PF (ZAPU) candidate was murdered, several other people were killed and many houses were burnt to the ground. In Kwe Kwe a PF (ZAPU) supporter who was being beaten up by Mugabe supporters managed to escape to a nearby police station where he asked for assistance. The rampaging mob demanded that the police hand him over to them; the police, in their cowardice, did so and he was beaten to death. No action was ever taken against the police or the murderers. Only after the violence had been going on for four days did Mugabe make any attempt to quell it.

This post-election violence was directly attributable to Mugabe's speech on national television, and his refusal to step in to stop it should have warned me of his capacity for using violence for both punishment and intimidation. During that week CCJP had appealed to the outgoing Minister of Home Affairs and the Commissioner of Police to stop the violence, but to no avail. At the time I was very angry with Mugabe over his speech and was sure that he could have stopped the violence had he wanted to – yet somehow tried to believe that he was understandably angry over the results and not yet aware of the extent of the violence. I was blinded by my respect for him.

The 1985 election was to set the pattern for subsequent elections, with violence occurring whenever an opposition party challenged ZANU (PF). The violence in the 1990 elections, however, took a different form. For the first time state agents in the CIO and uniformed police were directly involved. It was the first election for the Executive Presidency and for this election a new party had emerged, the Zimbabwe Unity Movement (ZUM) led by Edgar Tekere, the erstwhile secretary general of ZANU (PF). He had been dismissed by the party after making disparaging comments about the obviously falling standards of living. ZUM attracted several former members of the ruling party, including Patrick Kombayi, a former mayor of Gweru, who had been expelled from the party because he was too corrupt. He had remained popular in the area, however, and presented a real threat to Simon Muzenda, the Vice-President, in whose constituency he stood. Several days before the election, Kombayi was shot and very seriously wounded. One of his drivers was shot in the same incident. Both shootings were carried out by CIO agents in full view of the uniformed police. When two officers were charged with the offence later, they were convicted and subsequently pardoned by Mugabe along with many others who had been convicted of violence during the campaign. CCJP reacted strongly to both the shootings and later to the pardons. One of the pardons granted was to a group of ZANU (PF) youth. They had severely beaten a member of CCJP, who had been recording events in the run-up to the election, as many of its members were doing throughout the country at the time. Before their trial, Minister Nathan Shamuyarira offered to pay for their defence and whatever fine they might incur. This showed the ruling party's complete disregard of the rule of law when it came to protecting the party interests. Enoch Dumbutshena the courageous former Chief Justice, said that the President had 'given licence to members of ZANU (PF) and the CIO to kill opponents in the knowledge that they would be pardoned afterwards'. Subsequently Dumbutshena led another opposition party, the Forum Party. It attracted many academics and, perhaps unfortunately, many whites. The party was short lived, however, as it was infiltrated and destroyed by ZANU agents, and did not make any serious impact on the political scene. It did, however, open a debate on Zimbabwean democracy that continues still.

Another pattern established after the 1985 and subsequent elections was that of granting amnesty to all perpetrators of political violence before, during and after the elections. As this violence was caused almost exclusively by ZANU (PF) supporters, the first amnesty granted should have warned me that in Mugabe's mind violence was simply an electoral tool. His determination to retain power, regardless of the means or the cost, was very clear.

After the 1985 election the CCJP became more and more concerned about the increasing number of reports received of torture being applied routinely on suspects, mainly in the areas affected by *Gukurahundi*, although similar reports were coming in of torture in police and CIO stations throughout the country. A meeting I had with a senior CIO administrator about torture in the infamous Stops Camp in Bulawayo, and the commission's monitoring of the ongoing situation in Matabeleland as a whole, revealed that many people were being tortured severely, even in their homes and in front of their families – this in itself is a form of torture and intimidatory for the witnesses. We were also receiving many reports of suspects held in remand cells being tortured by investigating officers, and of many innocent people being detained by the CIO and subjected to severe torture, particularly in Stops Camp and the Esigodini and Gwanda Police Camps. The torture took many forms. Some was plain brutality, such as beating with sticks or fists, and kicking and beating the soles of the feet. Some was more refined, such as the use of electric shocks, often on nipples and genitals, and the use of water to partially drown the victim. The victims, whatever their sex, were completely naked, handcuffed and often leg-ironed. The most notorious torture camps were Balagwe in Matobo where hundreds – perhaps thousands – were tortured, the Esigodini police cells, Stops Camp in Bulawayo and the CIO station in Goromonzi.

Clearly a very serious situation pertained, and not only in Matabeleland, although that area was by far the worst. In December 1985, after Amnesty International had released its report on torture in Zimbabwe, a report that enraged the minister, who thought that the CCJP had been the source of the information, I was summoned, with Bishop Mutume and the new Director, Nicholas Ndebele, to a meeting with the new Home Affairs Minister, Enos Nkala,[1] an Ndebele who was a senior member of ZANU (PF). Nkala was extremely hostile throughout the meeting, threatening to imprison and deport us. Considering that we were all Zimbabwean born that was ridiculous, as he well knew. That meeting was strange in that we all felt threatened but at the same time we could not help our laughter when we were safely out of the building. Nkala was such a pompous little man. In Parliament after the meeting he made this statement in reference to the Amnesty International report:

> These statements, Mr Speaker, unequivocally suggest that the Zimbabwe Government instructs and has knowledge of alleged torture in police camps and prisons. Mr Speaker, these allegations display a totally negative view of the whole issue.

Nkala requested, or rather ordered us to inform him of the instances of torture that we had claimed were taking place. This we agreed to do and during 1986 we compiled a report that was published the following year. The day after our meeting with Nkala, however, the United States Ambassador had a meeting with him to discuss the same topic. This was most unfortunate for us, as Nkala was now convinced that we had communicated our fears to the US government as well, which we had not done. Of course, it was not true either that we had supplied information to Amnesty International, although we had confirmed their information before the report was published. These clashes with Nkala led to the arrest of Nick Ndebele in May 1986, which in turn led to my next encounter with Mugabe.

When Nick was detained, our attorneys worked hard to secure his release. First, they persuaded the High Court to order that Nick be brought to court each day to ensure that he was not subjected to torture. Those court appearances were to witness the solidarity of the church with the CCJP, as many of the clergy and religious, in their habits or vestments, attended the hearings. This sign of solidarity resulted in the Minister of Justice, Eddison Zvogbo, summoning one of the religious and me as we were waiting for the court to convene, and accusing us of embarrassing him and government with these demonstrations. After about 10 days the attorneys succeeded in having Nick freed.

As soon as the Court had ordered Nick's release for lack of evidence against him, I whisked him away to our home in Chinhoyi. The following morning I took him back to Harare and lodged him with the Apostolic pro-Nuncio who, though somewhat uncomfortable with the arrangement, agreed to keep him secure for the day. At about midday, two uniformed policemen appeared in my office. They asked me where Nick was and I pretended that I did not know. 'In that case,' they said, 'you are under arrest.' When I asked them to produce the warrant, I discovered I was being charged with 'being in possession of subversive documents'. In the hour or so that followed, while the police waited for a vehicle, I was able to phone Di and brief her on the situation, and took a call from the Misereor Africa Desk Officer (CCJP donor partners) whom I also told and urged him to 'spread the word'. Finally, we set off in the company of my attorney, Bryant Elliott, but not to the police station. Instead, I was driven out to my home in Chinhoyi for a search of the house.

Anticipating just such a situation, Di had frantically sorted and removed from the house any documents that could be regarded as subversive. She had also rung all the children to tell them what had happened, and they all came home, with Stephen 'roaring' home on his motorbike from Mvurwi. Before I arrived with the police Di had managed to contact all the media, especially the overseas press and radio (BBC made the announcement almost before the police arrived at the house), and all the human rights organisations, such as Amnesty International, and the Development Agencies in Europe, England and Ireland. Bishop Helmut Reckter was also very concerned and once the police had arrived and started their search he arrived in full regalia, and found one policeman had a son at St Ignatius. This man very quickly started apologising to the Bishop. The search did continue, however, and at one stage they were keen to take the family's passports away, but in the end did not. The two policemen involved in this act were suddenly distracted by the sight of Stephen walking around behind them with a tape recorder. When questioned, he said: 'Yes, I am recording everything you say, and when we go to court I will use it.' I managed to take the recorder away and to reassure them that it was not working, and Di lessened the tension by announcing that tea and sandwiches were ready in the dining-room. The house search revealed nothing, and I was then driven to Harare Central Police Station, where I found that Nick had already arrived. Hearing of my arrest, he had gone down to the police station to give himself up. So we were both in the cells for some hours that night – an experience I shall long remember.

Unbeknown to me, Di had decided to phone Mugabe. She first contacted his sister Sabina, whom I had helped to leave Rhodesia in 1978 and who was acquainted with Di. In her work in the Zvimba area – Mugabe's home area – Di had come to know his mother Bona and his sisters Sabina and Brigitte. Sabina gave Di her brother's phone number, but warned Di that President Nyerere of Tanzania was visiting, so Mugabe would probably not be able to speak to her. Di phoned and spoke to an aide, who reiterated the impossibility of speaking to the Prime Minister. Di stressed the urgency of the matter and asked simply that he be given the message that she had phoned. She was told that a return call was unlikely, but a few minutes later the phone rang and a voice said, 'This is Robert Mugabe.' Di, feeling that he could not possibly be responsible for or know of my arrest, told him what had happened and urged to him to have me released. He answered that he had heard of my arrest earlier in the evening and had already ordered my release. When he heard that I was still in custody, he said he would attend to it immediately – which indeed he did, for at about 11.30 that night both Nick and I were released. This action by Mugabe caused Minister Nkala, who ordered our arrests, to offer his resignation, which unfortunately was not accepted.

..... Margaret, Di, myself and Nick Ndebele, after release from Harare Central.

It still seems astonishing to me that a Prime Minister of any country would take a late night phone call and act on it immediately when it was on behalf of someone who was actively collecting evidence about the atrocities committed by his government and army. It was all the more amazing considering that he had so important a visitor with him at the time. I have always taken this gesture as an act of friendship, and this added to the confusion in my thoughts and feelings about him. This was, after all, 1986 and *Gukurahundi* had been in progress for more than three years. He knew how involved I was with what was taking place in Matabeleland; he must have felt that I was a threat to him and yet he ordered my release. That was difficult for me to understand and left me with the belief that he appreciated what I was doing but found it difficult to call for constraint in the 'dissident' offensive without appearing to be weakening.

On 22 December the conflict in Matabeleland ended with the signing of the Unity Accord between ZANU (PF) and PF (ZAPU). After long and tortuous negotiations, in which Nick Ndebele and myself had played a 'shuttle diplomacy' role whenever talks broke down, Mugabe attained what he had set out to achieve through *Gukurahundi* – the capitulation of Joshua Nkomo and his party and their absorption into ZANU (PF). The Unity Accord ended the violence in Matabeleland, but it also effectively created a one-party-state. Nkomo joined Muzenda as one of the two Vice Presidents. But the accord brought no economic or political benefit to the people of Matabeleland, who had suffered so grievously at the hands of the Fifth Brigade and the National Army for so long. Nor was any apology ever made to them for their extended suffering. At the end of 1987, Mugabe became the Executive President of Zimbabwe, the Head of State and Government, and the Commander in Chief of the Armed Forces.

Notes

1   After the 1985 election, when Mugabe announced his cabinet, I wrote to warn him that Enos Nkala was not a good choice.

CHAPTER 14

A Changing World

The year 1990 must have been a difficult year for Robert Mugabe. Major transformations were taking place in the world. Eastern European socialism was dead and there were great changes in the Soviet Union. On the home front, Zimbabweans fully expected constitutional changes that would usher in a one-party state. The CCJP was deeply concerned, as the history of one-party states was not glorious. We held a workshop, debated the pros and cons of the issue and agreed on a statement to the press urging government not to take this step. The newspaper chose to publish the statement on the day before Independence Day, the day on which we expected Mugabe to make an announcement about the one-party state. Instead, in his Independence Day speech he railed at the commission, accusing it of interference in political processes that were not within the ambit of religious duties. The announcement was not made, and later that year the ruling party rejected the idea of legislating for that form of government.

It was becoming clear at this time that the economic policies of Mugabe's government were not bearing fruit in terms of the investment needed in the country, and that the government had to do something radical in order to continue implementing its development plans. This led ultimately to an association with the World Bank and the International Monetary Fund (IMF), which brought the Economic Structural Adjustment Programme (ESAP) into being in the country. I believe that agreeing to ESAP must have been one of the most difficult decisions that Mugabe the socialist, the Marxist/Leninist, had ever made. The programme was applied half-heartedly and with great reluctance, but its negative effects altered Mugabe's political profile. As always with the involvement of the World Bank and the IMF, the poorest people suffered first and most, through the loss of employment opportunities, the removal of subsidies and the loosening of price controls. Over the following few years this led to a sharp decline in the popularity for the ruling party.

Transforming the economy from socialist to capitalist must have hurt Mugabe quite seriously. He had always proclaimed his Marxism/Leninism and he surely believed in it. This apparent 'about face' must have been a serious personal setback. And it is also clear now that the implementation of ESAP in Zimbabwe accelerated the growth of corruption in the country.

I met Mugabe again during 1990. At one of his pre-election 'meet the people' gatherings I expressed the commission's concern that the state of emergency, instituted by the Smith government in 1965, was still in force some 25 years later. The state of emergency had allowed many grave violations of human rights over the years, including detention without trial, mandatory sentences, torture and even murder committed 'in good faith'. Since I had spoken and written on this topic quite often, Mugabe responded to me, or rather to the gathering, with a good-humoured 'This is Mike's hobbyhorse this year. He always has hobbyhorses' – which drew a laugh from the audience, but Mugabe did not answer my question. The state of emergency ended that year, and Di and I had a celebration dinner with many friends and acquaintances.

Part of my dilemma was the on-going confusion caused by the personal interaction I had with Mugabe during the 1990s. We met again at the sad occasion of the death of his first wife Sally in 1992. Sally had been much loved by the people of Zimbabwe and had dedicated the last years of her life to working with underprivileged children through the Child Survival and Development Foundation, of which she was patron. Bishop Mutume and I went to Zimbabwe House, Mugabe's residence, to pay our respects and to express our sadness at her passing. Mugabe appeared sad and distracted at this brief meeting, but clearly appreciated the gesture. Di and I called on him again on the day before the funeral, when Sally was lying in state in the residence, and again he seemed to appreciate our being there.

A year later I met Mugabe at the Catholic Cathedral in Harare, where he was attending a memorial service for Brother Arthur Dupuis FMS, my revered predecessor in the CCJP. At that time I was (and still am) concerned about the conflict in the Sudan and, knowing that Mugabe was preparing to attend the Commonwealth Heads of Government Meeting (CHOGM) in Cyprus, I had prepared a letter for him[1] in case I did not get the opportunity to speak to him. Prior to Mass I gave the letter to the priest celebrating Mass, and as we came out of the cathedral he handed it to Mugabe, who looked around for me, asking: 'Where is Mike?' When he saw me he came over to me, took my hand and led me to his car. He got into the back seat of the Mercedes and invited me to sit with him, which I did. We sat close to one another and, with the President of Zimbabwe holding my hand, we discussed the topic for some minutes. Then I wished him a pleasant journey and left. Again the warmth of relationship, which I had felt so often before, affected me.

The fact that nothing arose as a result of my suggestions, and that Sudan was not even mentioned at CHOGM in their concluding press release, did not in any way cause me to doubt Mugabe's sincerity. He had appeared to be interested in my concern and was keen to hear what I might suggest that he did at CHOGM.

I attended many other public functions that were addressed by Mugabe and I was always impressed by his bearing and by what he said. It seemed to me that he always struck the right note and never waffled. So over the years my respect for him grew, even as late as 1994, when he was the guest of honour at the centenary celebrations of the Dominican Sisters in Zimbabwe. He spoke with extraordinary insight about the churches' role in promoting the morality of the nation and I came away amazed and saddened by the contradiction between the man's life and his words.

I also had business meetings with Mugabe in the run-up to the Presidential elections in 1990 and 1996, during his series of 'meet the people' gatherings with various groups in society. At the second such meeting during the 1996 election campaign I pointed out how disappointed I was at the return of racist reporting in the government-controlled media, evident particularly in *The Sunday Mail*, which had begun to print racist advertisements and articles (this after an advertisement in *The Sunday Mail* placed by Francis Boka, a businessman, which talked of crocodiles and pythons in reference to the white community). His response to me was terse; he had not seen any 'reverse racism' in the press – a brief insight into 'another Mugabe'.

Notes

1 My letter to Mugabe on Sudan expressed my deep concern over the fact that the war had already being going on for 30 years, that it was a religious and racial war and that the government of Sudan actively supported slavery. I believed that the Commonwealth body had a responsibility to take some action to bring stability to that country.

CHAPTER 15

Land – A Political Ploy

Since the beginning of colonisation land has been a major bone of contention. Although the colonists of the country that became Southern Rhodesia came in search of gold, it was soon clear that gold was not readily to be found and many people turned to agriculture, taking over the land from the people and, through legislation, ensuring that the people would become the 'workers' on the land. The early wars of liberation, known as the Mashona and Matabele rebellions, or the First *Chimurenga* (war of liberation), aimed to rid the land of the occupiers. But the indigenous people lost those wars and the land remained in the hands of the colonisers. The Land Apportionment Act passed in the 1930s and the Land Tenure Act of 1970 ensured that the black population was confined to 'reserves' or 'Tribal Trust Lands', except for those required for labour in the towns and cities. These pieces of legislation were ostensibly to protect the majority and to ensure that sufficient land was available to them, but a good portion of the land remained as state land and was subsequently settled by white farmers. The 'native' land became increasingly overworked and overgrazed, so that black agriculture became subsistence agriculture, with the farming families often depending on assistance from their wage-earning relatives in the urban areas. The second war of liberation from the early 1960s to the end of the 1970s had, as one of its primary objectives, the freeing of the land for the people.

One would have expected, therefore, that reclaiming and redistributing the land would have been a high priority for Mugabe's government. The

Lancaster House agreement made the appropriation of land dependent upon the landowner being willing to sell and the government being willing to buy: the 'willing buyer – willing seller' concept. The farmers expected land reform in 1980, and for the white farming population, particularly the commercial farmers who had owned and farmed the land for two or three generations, the threat of expropriation was a cause for real concern.

It must be said that efforts were made early in the 1980s to appropriate and redistribute the land, quite legitimately under the Lancaster House agreement, but the land affected tended to be land abandoned during the war or land expropriated from absentee landowners. However, apart from a few minor, and indeed temporary, successes in those settlements where irrigation had been laid on, the newly acquired land became no better than the communal lands where the majority of the black population lived.

The failure of these efforts can be put down to the lack of planning, the lack of government interaction with the farmers themselves, the lack of funds for fertiliser and seed, the lack of extension services and a lack of necessary equipment, such as tractors, ploughs and piping. In many cases, where there was infrastructure on the farm being resettled – such as barns, workshops, houses, storerooms, schools and clinics – this was dismantled so that the new farmers could use the building material for their own houses. Without guidance and without capital or credit facilities 'destruction preceded construction'. Where there were insufficient materials for all the newcomers, the trees were cut down for building houses, and for sale as firewood to supplement the farmers' income. The resulting deforestation was devastating. In many instances, peasant farmers who had been given land on formerly commercial farms found they could not make a living and returned to their old homes in the communal areas where they had a supportive community around them.

After the initial appropriation of land, the steam went out of the resettlement effort and land appeared to have been put on to the government's back burner. However, if a landowner wished to sell land, it had to be offered to the government first; if the government wanted the land it was purchased – if not, the land could be sold elsewhere, but only after the government had issued a certificate of 'no further interest' in the land. By 1999 over 80% of the land owned by commercial farmers had been purchased since independence, with the approval of the government as expressed in their certificate of 'no further interest' – which makes a lie of the government's subsequent claim that it was 'reclaiming the land stolen from our grandfathers by the colonists'.

The government's initial approach to land redistribution was viewed with relief by the commercial farmers. They continued farming as before, feeling more secure than perhaps they had in the past. At the same time, the Save the Children Fund of the United Kingdom (SCF(UK)) initiated its Farm Worker Programme to encourage farmers to improve the living and working conditions of farmworkers. Built on the successful SCF(UK) Farm Health Worker Programme, this programme proved to be very effective and many farmers began to improve workers' houses and water supply, to build pre-schools, primary schools and small clinics or dispensaries. SCF(UK) subsequently helped to set up a Zimbabwean NGO, the Farm Community Trust of Zimbabwe (FCTZ), to continue the work and to take the programme to other areas of the country.

It must be said, also, that the Commercial Farmers' Union (CFU) tried on several occasions to assist government in resettling land that was available for resettlement and that many commercial farmers whose land bordered the Communal Areas assisted their neighbours with inputs and equipment to improve the cropping ability of the communal farmer, some with great success. One of the beneficiaries of such co-operation was Border Gezi, a ZANU (PF) MP who farmed a smallholding in the Mount Darwin area, north of Harare. He brought his tractor to a local commercial farmer for servicing and repair whenever needed. Gezi later became the Governor of Mashonaland Central and subsequently died in a road accident.

It is clear that at independence the commercial farmers in Zimbabwe were the backbone of the economy. Having been through the sanctions era under the Smith government, they had learned to diversify and intensify their production. By the late 1990s agriculture had become of even greater importance to the economy, with many of these commercial farmers achieving very high standards of production for both food and cash crops. Collectively, they were also the single highest employer, apart from the government. With some 350 000 workers on the farms in 1976, as well as their wives and families, more than a million people were dependent on the commercial farmers for their livelihood. By the mid-1980s this number had grown to 1,7 million. The farmers generated wealth and particularly, foreign currency, which was so desperately needed in this landlocked country.

While the issue of land was initially placed low down on the government's priority list, the ruling party continued to use the skewed ownership of land as an election ploy. At each election it would announce that land was a priority and would be dealt with to the benefit of the people if the party were returned to power, but it was not until 1992 that any new legislation on land was promulgated. The 1992 Land Acquisition Bill was intended to assure the people that land was still a priority for government, but it was a most dangerous piece of legislation, giving enormous power to the Minister of Lands and Agriculture, denying landowners access to the courts and laying the land redistribution process open to corruption.

The CCJP severely criticised the legislation before it was read in Parliament and succeeded in having some aspects changed. In a document on land reform published by the commission in 1995, it said of the 1992 Act and clause 6 of Amendment 11 of the Constitution of Zimbabwe (1990):[1]

> This amendment has culminated in the promulgation of the Land Acquisition Act in its present form providing for the designation, acquisition and compensation of land without recourse to the court where the question of fairness of compensation is in dispute. This particular denial of the most basic natural principle of law leads one to conclude that the Land Acquisition Act of 1992 combined with clause 6 of the Constitution of Zimbabwe Amendment No 11 of 1990 is bad law and is a gross violation of individual rights.

When the amended Bill became law, 116 farms were immediately acquired and redistributed – not to the land-hungry masses in the communal farming areas, however, but to senior party members and civil servants. This gross corruption was to cause the British Government, quite understandably, to suspend its payments to the resettlement fund. Later when things went seriously wrong, the British were blamed for the fact that the resettlement programme had failed.

These farms were allocated to 'party cronies' at a time when Mugabe was out of the country, and on his return he demanded angrily in one of his State of the Nation addresses to Parliament that the names of the farms allocated and of those who had acquired them be published in Hansard and that the farms be returned to the resettlement programme. The names were indeed subsequently published, but the farms were not returned to the programme. When asked about this a few years later, Mugabe flippantly announced that this was the start of a new resettlement programme, involving 'black commercial farmers'. This was the corruption about which CCJP had warned before the Bill was read in Parliament and it was gradually becoming clear to me that the President was using his patronage to maintain his power base.

At this time, the Land Act was used also against black people, in both communal and private land ownership. One example of the communal ownership violation was the dispossession of the Tangwena people from the land they had settled after returning from exile at the end of the war. The Smith government had accused Chief Tangwena and his people of harbouring and assisting terrorists and had attempted to force the chief and the people to move from their lands by taking their children from them and placing them in various schools throughout the country. The chief courageously stood his ground until the children were returned – then he led his people into exile in Mozambique. When they returned they reoccupied the land they had left, which had, in the mean time, been designated as forestry land. The chief asked various ministers at the time if it was acceptable for them to settle there once again and had been assured that it was. However, in the early 1990s, some years after the old chief had died, the police arrived at their settlement early one morning and evicted the people without any warning, to claim the land for Didymus Mutasa, a very senior party official. CCJP was approached to take up the case and to find food and shelter for the people in the interim – which was done – but the people were never allowed back onto that land.

Another example of this misuse of the land legislation was the harassment of Reverend Ndabaningi Sithole, who was by then well over 70. He had bought a farm on the outskirts of Harare known as Churu Farm. As there was a large and growing shortage of housing in Harare, he set aside a portion of the land which he divided into plots and allowed people to rent these plots and build houses. About 3 000 families had taken advantage of Sithole's offer; many houses had been built and many more were being constructed. Then one morning in November 1993, the riot police arrived and began evicting people from their homes, informing them that the building of houses there was illegal – they would have to move. Sithole and some of the Churu residents came to see me and described what had happened. The CCJP took the matter to court and obtained a temporary interdict to stop the evictions. Our Legal Officer Elizabeth Feltoe and other CCJP staff worked tirelessly to take and record affidavits from more than 600 people to back our court application to prevent further evictions. By the time we had received the court order and had gone to the farm, several thousand people had been evicted and were milling

..... *The Churu Farm evictions.*

around on the side of the road, surrounded by their furniture and belongings and trying to set up shelters against the threatening rain.

The commission's solicitor Bryant Elliott and I approached the riot police, but they were unwilling to talk to us. We pointed out that we had obtained a court order and that the people should be allowed back to their homes. After some haggling, the police allowed the people to go back, but on the following day, a Saturday, they were again evicted. I received a phone call at about 10 o'clock and Bryant and I went to the farm again and insisted that the police allow the people to go back to their homes. After an hour or so of shuttling between the various senior policemen, the people were given permission to go back. Satisfied that all was now well, we went home. An hour later they were evicted again, and this time the police would not allow us into the area. The farm was later 'designated'[2] by the government and Sithole was evicted. In all about Z$3 000 000 worth of buildings and other materials that had been used by people hungry for homes had been destroyed – homes that the government could not supply. The commission subsequently compiled a booklet of the whole Churu tragedy, and later commissioned a socio-economic study on urban housing, or the lack of it.

.....*With our attorney, Bryant Elliott (second from right), at Churu.*

As the decade of the 1990s drew to a close, land once again became the focus of the ruling party's attempt to revitalise its waning support. At that time a new force appeared on the Zimbabwean scene – the 'war veterans', of whom more will be said later. But this development showed Mugabe a way in which this new force could be used to bolster his now faltering party and policies. They were also used with devastating effect in the all-out assault on the commercial farmers that took place later.

Notes

1   The Land Question, Maposa, 1995 ISBN: 0 7974 1525 4.
2   The Land Acquisition Act of 1992 provided for the designation of land that the government intended to acquire. This meant, among other things, that the land could not be sold once it had been designated.

CHAPTER 16

Laying the Foundations of a Dictatorship

The momentous changes in Eastern Europe in the early 1990s negatively affected Mugabe, his party and his plan for a one-party state. There were also changes taking place in Africa, the most notable of which was the transformation of South Africa and the emergence of Nelson Mandela. This was to affect Mugabe, the person and the politician, adversely. President Mandela replaced Mugabe in the list of world favourites and the focus of world aid shifted to the new 'Rainbow nation'. It should be remembered that ZANU (PF) supported the South African Pan-Africanist Congress (PAC), which did not endear it to the African National Congress (ANC), the new ruling party in South Africa led by Mandela. While superficially there was great friendship between the two countries in the early 1990s, I believe that this may well have contributed to Mugabe's determination to strengthen his own position at home.

The decade of the 1990s saw great movement on the Zimbabwean constitutional front that was to lead to the first electoral defeat experienced by the ruling party some years later. The constitution agreed on at Lancaster House in November 1979 was designed to take the country through the first decade of independence, and thereafter it was generally expected that a new constitution would be drawn up, in which the people could direct the future path of the nation. The government, however, having altered the Constitution 14 times by 1990, without any consultation with the people, produced the type of constitution that suited its purposes well and which was very much in its interests to keep.

In 1987, in accordance with the Lancaster House agreement, the 20 seats in Parliament reserved for the white population had fallen away and the Senate had been abandoned. Two Acts of Parliament were passed – the Electoral Act and the Presidential Powers Act. Under the former, the total number of seats was increased to 150, of which 10 were reserved for traditional chiefs elected by the Chiefs' Council, eight created for the newly established provincial governors, who also had cabinet status, and 12 left for the President to bestow, ostensibly to represent sectors of society otherwise unrepresented, such as the disabled. The Presidential Powers Act made provision for an Executive Presidency. The two Acts in effect guaranteed the ruling party's perpetuity in power, the additional seats making it nearly impossible to unseat it. At any future election an opposition party would be required not only to win a simple majority, but to win by more than 30 seats, failing which the President in his selection of the 20 unelected seats could retain a majority in Parliament.

I believe the political consequences of the Unity Accord and the creation of the Executive Presidency to have been a major step in the wrong direction for the country, for several reasons. It took Mugabe out of Parliament, where he had been able to interact with MPs, to see and hear them in the House, to know those who were performing well and those who were not. It had also enabled him to form his own opinion of the efficacy of his ministers and the government as a whole. As Executive President he would have to rely on briefings from his ministers, their secretaries, his intelligence services and the police, briefings that did not necessarily paint an accurate picture. The creation of the Executive Presidency also took him away from the common people, except when he was addressing rallies, at which it was impossible for anyone to speak out against the government.

The executive nature of the presidency made Mugabe, the individual, extremely powerful and the subsequent promulgation of the Presidential Powers Act made him almost unassailable. In 1990 the presidency was to become a six-year term of office, which ensured that even if the ruling party lost an election, its leader would remain as the President for at least a year after the lost election. This together with the Presidential Powers Act would make it impossible for any other party to govern. The effect of this law became evident in the 2000 parliamentary elections.

Between 1980 and 1999 some 17 changes were made to the Constitution, most of them reducing the protection of human rights and undermining democracy. Much new legislation also made a wider democracy harder to attain. The Electoral Act and the Presidential Powers Act were but two of these new controls imposed on the country. The University of Zimbabwe (Amendment) Act brought the University under more direct control of the government, and the Private Voluntary Organisations Act gave the government wide powers to control, or even to take over, any such organisation that it thought was violating any part of the Act. The government did not require any evidence in this regard; the opinion of a minister was sufficient. When added to the continued control of the mass media, particularly national radio to which most people had access, these controls began to make it extremely difficult for the people to be informed of the truth of the situation in the country.

While each of these controls, when enacted, caused concern to those who would be affected by them, it was not until rather too late that civil society players began to understand the government's determination to maintain its control. Even at that stage we gravely underestimated the danger the country now faced. Add to all this the facts that Mugabe was the leader, Prime Minister and President who allowed, perhaps ordered, these things to happen and that he was undoubtedly responsible for *Gukurahundi* and its tragic consequences. I should have been aware much earlier that we were ruled by a tyrant who would be satisfied with nothing less than totalitarian control.

CHAPTER 17

National Constitutional Assembly

In 1996, as the situation in the country was clearly deteriorating, both politically and economically, the Zimbabwe Council of Churches' Justice, Peace and Reconciliation desk convened a meeting of the major players in civil society, including the Trade Union Congress, church organisations, human rights groups and women's groups to discuss the reasons for this deterioration. After several meetings it became abundantly clear that the Constitution was seriously faulty and that under the current dispensation the country could not move forward politically or economically. Out of these meetings the National Constitutional Assembly (NCA) emerged. This was a national movement that included all of the major players in society, except the ruling party, which had declined to join on the grounds that the Constitution was a government affair in which the public should not meddle. The NCA was determined to bring about a new Constitution, designed by the people, that would ensure greater democracy in the political arena, stability in the country and a more conducive investment climate.

The NCA began to work on a new Constitution led by a Task Force chaired by a veteran trade union leader, Morgan Tsvangirai, who was later to mount the first viable challenge to Mugabe and his party. I served as his Vice-Chairperson, representing the interests of the churches in the constitutional process. Staff members were recruited and office space rented. Then the real work began, to make the wider public aware of the need for and the benefits of a new Constitution, to collect their views and begin to formulate the provisions of this new dispensation. This work was to lead to the first defeat Mugabe and his party had experienced since coming to power.

Over the next two years, the NCA organised several street demonstrations objecting to certain government actions; also in promotion of the constitutional work being done by the NCA or in support of other important issues. The demonstrations, which took the form of marches through the main streets of the cities, served to re-awaken the political interest of the people who had all but given up hope of any meaningful change, and at the outset they were well attended. It was always necessary to obtain permission from the police to hold a demonstration and permission would be given in most cases. They were, however, carefully monitored by the riot police and when it became obvious to government that the marches were strengthening the resolve of the people to bring about constitutional change, the police were ordered to step in and stop them. Accordingly when the police refused permission for a demonstration already planned, a running shuttle ensued between the organisers of the marches, the courts and the police. The organisers would petition the courts for a ruling allowing a peaceful demonstration, the courts would issue the necessary court order, the public would assemble at the starting point of the demonstration and the police would arrive with their batons, shields and tear-gas. Sometimes they would allow the march to begin and would then wade in with batons or tear-gas to break it up, sending people reeling in all directions to form up again somewhere else and be beaten again.

However, when it became clear to government and to the police that the demonstrations were becoming demonstrably more popular events, the police became far more serious and violent in their breaking up of the marches. They paid scant attention to the court orders allowing the demonstrations, showing complete contempt for the courts, and simply ignored the efforts of court officials to enforce the orders.

Many of the human rights groups, trade unions, political parties – of which there were several – the churches and the general public took part in these marches. First at the scene would be Isaac Maposa, the Director of the NCA, Tsvangirai, the Chairperson, and me, his Vice-Chairperson.

But we would not be alone for long, as the people gathered quite quickly, vainly hoping that the march would get underway before the police arrived. Members of my family were always prominent, especially as we are all rather large, and as we all felt very strongly about the issue at stake were very active in encouraging protesters. Many other faces became familiar as the marches continued. Lovemore Madhuku (later Chairperson of the NCA), Tendai Biti and Edwina and Newton Spicer were always there – a couple who filmed every political occasion and kept records of all the activities. Edwina had made the documentary film of the history of CCJP and several others on the media and the activities of the NCA and later of the new political party. Others included Geoff Feltoe, Sister Judith Jackson OP and many of the local and foreign press. Brenda Burrell and Keith Goddard, representing the gay community, were also very faithful in attending. They had been fighting for a few years for recognition of their rights and had been the objects of a presidential diatribe at the International Book Fair, which Mugabe had opened in 1998. By far the majority of the marchers, however, would be the unnamed, courageous people who took part despite the beatings and the tear gas, to register their anger at the activities of government.

I was away when one such march took place and Di and my sons Stephen and Michael were involved in a tussle with the police. Very soon after the march had set off from the normal starting point in Central Avenue, the riot police arrived and set about the marchers. At Di's suggestion the marchers went into the cathedral grounds, hoping that the premises would offer some protection, only to find the cathedral doors locked. However the porch, with its two large, wrought-iron clips for the open doors were used to form a cordon around Isaac and Stephen, who had had an altercation with a particular policeman during the march. The police followed the marchers in and tried unsuccessfully to arrest them. As long as the cordon held they could not pull either of them out. That caused a short cessation of activities while the police decided what to do and the marchers sent for the parish priest, who came, albeit unwillingly, and persuaded the police through Michael, my son, to withdraw from the cathedral grounds. Reluctantly they eventually did this, and as they clambered into their vehicle, complaining loudly, they became aware that the driver of the truck was unable to get it started, to the great amusement of the harassed marchers. To the embarrassment of the police, several of the marchers in high spirits gave their vehicle a push and finally got it going amid laughter, cheers and jeers.

In the early marches there was even some light-hearted banter between the marchers and the police, but later things became much more serious and at one particular march the trouble began in earnest. By this time the war veterans had become a force and when our march had reached the centre of town, the marchers were met by a howling mob of club and stone-carrying veterans who had marched together from the ZANU (PF) headquarters and now proceeded to wade into them and hurt several people, one of them quite seriously. When the two marches clashed, I was towards the back and as I came around the corner I watched the police actually assisting the veterans to assault marchers and innocent bystanders. Tear gas was being used indiscriminately on marchers and bystanders, simply to disperse the crowd.

..... Di, Stephen and Mike jnr with Isaac Maphosa outside the Cathedral.

After this the NCA marches stopped for a time, but there were other marches to highlight particular issues, such as International Women's Day, Human Rights Day, Press Freedom Day and other similar commemorations. We took advantage of these days, as the police really did not wish to interfere with UN commemorative days. However, when the Law Society carried out its annual march, the police were there in full force and they forced us to move away from the front of the parliament buildings. In doing so one policeman came into physical contact with another very large white man, a senior advocate, Adrian de Bourbon, who successfully sued the Minister of Home Affairs for assault. He asked for no compensation but required an apology, which he received. This was the first demonstration to which the police brought their dogs and threatened to turn them on the marchers. There can be nothing more frightening to unarmed, peaceful protesters than excited Alsatians, straining at their leashes, further exacerbated by the taunts of the handlers. Fortunately the dogs were not unleashed.

The year 1998 proceeded with a great deal of constitutional work being done by the NCA. All over the country meetings and workshops were held to educate and inform the people about the failings of the current Constitution and the checks and balances needed to control government excesses, and to solicit people's own ideas for the new Constitution. I was involved in meetings with the commercial farming community, encouraging farmers to take an interest in the issue, asking them to ensure that their workers were educated about it and urging them to support the NCA. In my capacity as Director of the CCJP and Vice-Chairperson of the NCA Task Force, I addressed about 40 Farmers' Association meetings in the Mashonaland provinces and in some parts of Manicaland, speaking from the perspective of both democracy and human rights.

Members of the President's Office and the CIO attended many of these meetings and after the first couple of meetings I would tell the CIO men not to bother taking notes as I was making the same points at each meeting. For some reason this seemed to cause embarrassment to them. But they undoubtedly reported back on my talks and on the response of the farmers.

The commercial farmers generally and their union, the CFU, had always taken a non-partisan stand in the politics of the country. But now they responded well to the campaign, allowing the NCA onto their farms and giving it financial support.

During this period, the NCA tried on many occasions to gain access to the national broadcast media in order to reach and inform as many people as possible. Several advertising campaigns were developed for radio and television and we hoped to persuade the heads of the broadcast departments to run discussion programmes to assist people to understand the process and the importance of the exercise. Our efforts were unsuccessful, but the newspaper campaign through the courageous independent newspapers went ahead and a poster campaign ensured that there were posters on trees all over the country.

CHAPTER 18

Breaking the Silence

The year 1997 brought a feeling of frustration to the commission about the plight of the people of Matabeleland. Fourteen years after the presentation of CCJP's first report to Mugabe on the activities of Fifth Brigade, 12 years after the last report and a decade after the end of the hostilities in Matabeleland, no apology had been made by the government and no rehabilitative action had been taken to assuage the continued suffering of the people. After the Unity Accord in 1987, very little development had taken place in Matabeleland and the many thousands of surviving victims were left with their suffering ignored, not least because most Zimbabweans had no idea of the extent of the violence that had taken place.

In 1992, the publication of *Reaching for Justice* reminded the commission of the need for further research into the horror of those days, and the Bishops agreed that a comprehensive report should be compiled. Unfortunately CCJP at that time had neither the funds nor the staff to undertake so large a project. Then David Coltart, the LRF director, joined me and he sought finance and recruited the researchers. Work started on the report in 1995. Two courageous people who must remain nameless carried out the major part of the research and one of them compiled the report. The research entailed poring over all the newspaper reports of those years and assessing their truthfulness; it involved the interviewing of many hundreds of witnesses and the comparing of witness statements of the same incidents, and listening to some truly horrifying stories of rape, torture and murder committed by soldiers of the Fifth Brigade. The author regularly brought completed sections of the report to my office to check the facts and to ensure that nothing was published that was incorrect or could be challenged by the government (it is worth noting that since publication, the content of the report has never been challenged by anyone in government). This close collaboration with the author refocused my mind on the tragedy and atrocity of the Matabeleland massacres and Mugabe's role in them. It reminded me of the many violent statements he had made, as Prime Minister, while the events were occurring, and this played a part in changing my feelings for him.

Just two quotations from this report show the extraordinary callousness and violence of the Fifth Brigade during its operations in Matabeleland:

SOLOBONI 23 February 1983: Five Brigade rounded up entire village at the borehole. Six people were chosen at random and were bayoneted to death and buried in one grave. Everyone was then beaten. Five people were beaten to death and one person died years later, partly as a result of this beating. Another man who wept to see his brother killed was severely beaten and died a few weeks later from his injuries. One old lady who was found in her hut was raped, and 5 Bde then set fire to a plastic bag and burned the old lady with it, setting fire to her blanket. She died 3 weeks later from her burns. One hut was burned. (14 dead, 1 raped, 50 (estimated) beaten, 1 hut burnt)

MKHONYENI Feb 1983. All the villagers were forced to witness the burning to death of 26 villagers, in the three huts of Dhlamini. Women and children died. There was only one survivor ...[1]

By November 1996 the final draft of the report was ready to go to the Bishops' Conference for their approval. I had sent the draft to individual Bishops earlier that month and in December I met them all at their administrative meeting in Gweru. I was confident that they would approve the report and allow it to be published. Unfortunately Bishop Mutume, the CCJP President, was absent from the meeting. Archbishop Karlen CMM and Bishop Prieto of Hwange supported the publication, but the Apostolic

Delegate, Archbishop Peter Paul Prabhu, an ineffectual Roman diplomat, did not and neither did the Archbishop of Harare. The Bishops asked for some minor adjustments to be made, one of which was to produce a second document showing just the recommendations of the report. While this was completely unnecessary, it served the purpose of delaying the publication, allowing the Bishops time to consider the possible consequences and to decide on the safest route to take in the future. As I turned to the door to leave the room when the discussions were over, I heard Archbishop Chakaipa say something that I did not catch. He had made no contribution to the discussions at all, so I was somewhat surprised when he spoke at this late stage. However, I turned and asked him what he had said and he replied 'Never! This will never be published.' I did not take this as seriously as I should have, considering what occurred later, but believed that the majority of the Bishops would overrule him when the time came.

Among the report's recommendations were that a trust should be formed to raise and distribute development funds in the affected areas; that mass graves should be identified and, in consultation with the

..... Part of the team learning how to recover human remains from mass graves in Matabeleland.

communities, the bodies exhumed and reburied with cultural and religious rites; and that constitutional safeguards be put in place to ensure that the same horror could not be repeated in the future. We did not recommend that the government pay compensation for the damage done, but the report noted: 'The suppositionary damages listed above [referring to Part lll of the report headed 'Legal Damages'] which is far from a complete listing of likely damage suffered in the 1980s disturbances, already add up to US$68,162,000 or Z$661,125,000 at current exchange rates.' We hoped that this estimate of the damage done would show prospective donors the enormity of the human cost of *Gukurahundi*.

This report is without doubt the most comprehensive report of the gross human rights violations that took place in Matabeleland, and remains the most damning body of evidence against Mugabe, his party, the commander of the Fifth Brigade (now Air Marshal) Perence Shiri and those who carried out his orders. It allowed the people of the rest of the country to understand, for the first time, what had happened to the people of Matabeleland in the early 1980s.

Entitled *Breaking the Silence: Building True Peace*, this report was to create many difficulties for the Bishops' Conference and for myself, but its greatest impact would be on Mugabe as, for the first time a comprehensive, and accurate history of the Matabeleland offensive was available to the world at large. But more than that, the report offered concrete and manageable means of compensating and reconciling with the affected people. At the Bishops' Conference in February 1997 the Bishops agreed that the two documents should be printed and delivered to the President with a letter requesting a meeting with him on the matter. With this encouragement, we went ahead and printed 1 000 copies of the report and waited for the Bishops' approval.

Bishop Mutume and I delivered two copies each of the report and the recommendations to the President's office in March 1997 and received the signature of his private secretary. From that day to this Mugabe has not acknowledged receipt of the documents, although he has made reference to them on several occasions. And even after four letters on Bishops'

Conference letterheads and 69 phone calls to the President's office I was unable to secure a meeting between Mugabe and the Bishops.

In mid-1997 the LRF, then led by Eileen Sawyer, decided to go ahead and publish the report after it had been leaked to the *Mail & Guardian* in South Africa and had appeared on that website. I was in Europe at the time and so could not be held responsible for the decision to publish. I am still not aware who leaked the report but I am most grateful to whoever it was, because it meant there was no further point in withholding the document until it received the approval of the Bishops' Conference. That approval never came.

Many years after the events recounted in the report, forensic anthropologists from Argentina visited Zimbabwe and introduced the CCJP and Amani Trust, another human rights organisation, to the scientific methods of finding, recording and opening the graves of victims of the Matabeleland terror. The findings from the opening of five graves, one containing six bodies and four with three or more, vindicated the report. The reburials of the bodies after examination were carried out with religious and cultural rites that had a profound effect on the relatives of the dead and brought relief and closure for them. Unfortunately, the worsening situation in the country did not allow us to continue this exercise, but I hope that one day these ceremonies will be completed.

In November 1997 Father Pius Ncube became the Archbishop of Bulawayo and he played an important role in sanctifying the exhumations and blessing the reburials. His presence reassured the people that someone still cared about their suffering and was trying to put right whatever was possible. The Archbishop's extraordinary courage was to become very evident a year or so later when he stood firmly against the criminal violence, corruption and destruction brought about by Mugabe and ZANU (PF).

1997 was therefore a very important year for the Catholic Church in Zimbabwe, for the CCJP and for me. But the publication of the report affected negatively my relationship with the Bishops' Conference, which I had served almost continuously since 1978. I truly believed, and still do, that the church had in this document the truth of the Matabeleland atrocities and had a duty to expose it. I was bitterly disappointed by the Bishops' refusal to approve the report, which at the time I could not understand, as they had always relied on me to bring important issues to their attention and to deal with them. Now they were refusing to allow the truth to be told for reasons they would not share with me. After their refusal again in the June meeting, I went to a cottage we owned in Nyanga and agonised over this for several days, after which I wrote a letter to them emphatically expressing my distress and calling on them to reconsider their decision. I received no response to that letter, but thereafter there was a certain tension between me and the Conference that eventually led to my leaving the CCJP in September 1999.

Notes

1   The names of the author and the printers cannot be published for obvious reasons. The report was published by the Catholic Commission for Justice and Peace in Zimbabwe and the Legal Resources Foundation in Zimbabwe. It also appeared in the *Mail & Guardian* in South Africa.

The Road to Tyranny

PART THREE

CHAPTER 19

Things Fall Apart

It could be said that 1997 was the major turning point for Mugabe, in more ways than one. That was when the longstanding corruption in the government and the ruling party began to catch up with him. It had started towards the end of the 1980s, with the revelations, by Geoff Nyarota, courageous editor of the *Bulawayo Chronicle*. He disclosed that MPs and senior party members were abusing their right to purchase cars from Willowvale Motor Industries, Zimbabwe's only vehicle assembly plant. They had been allowed to buy cars for visiting their constituencies at a time when cars were in short supply, but after buying the vehicles at factory prices they then sold them at a huge profit.

Despite grave threats against him, Nyarota published the story in his newspaper in October 1988, which led to Mugabe setting up a commission of inquiry led by Mr Justice Sandura. The findings of the Sandura Commission were quite dramatic and led to even more dramatic consequences for those it implicated. Maurice Nyagumbo, a well-liked and respected senior party man, committed suicide, and Ministers Mutumbuka, Shava and Nkala resigned and were saved from prosecution by presidential pardon. Mutumbuka subsequently worked for the World Bank, Nkala disappeared from the political scene and Shava, after a year or so in the wilderness, returned to active politics in the Midlands.

The revelations over Willowvale, soon termed 'Willowgate', made Geoff Nyarota something of a media hero, working as he did for the government newspaper group, but it left the government in something of a quandary. It did not want its editor uncovering and publishing damning evidence against party luminaries, so he was promoted to a higher status but was given no office, no telephone and indeed no job. Obviously he could not continue there and he resigned. Subsequently he became the editor of a new paper, *The Daily News*, the only independent daily news-paper in Zimbabwe, which continued to expose government and ruling party misrule.

The Willowgate scandal was followed in 1993 by the corrupt distribu-tion of acquired farmland to senior party members which I mentioned earlier, the 'new kind of resettlement' – that of black commercial farmers. The fact that all the beneficiaries were senior party officials did not escape the notice of the public. The next major corruption incident to come to the attention of the public was the theft of some Z$480 million from the War Victims Compensation Fund. The Smith government had set up this fund as the 'Terrorist Victims Relief Fund', specifically for non-combatant victims of the war. At independence the name was changed and people – other than combatants – who could claim to have been harmed by the war in one way or another could claim compensation from the fund. Z$480 million was allocated to it by the 1994 budget, and the ransacking of the fund by the so-called 'war veterans', led by Dr Chenjerai 'Hitler' Hunzvi – whose medical qualifications were questionable – began soon after that. Starting with himself and his family, he examined anyone who wished to claim from the fund, finding varying degrees of disability. In these 'medi-cal' examinations, some serving members of government were found to be more than 100% disabled. When it was discovered that huge sums of money had been awarded to people, some of whom had no disability at all, a commission of inquiry was set up under Mr Justice (later Chief Justice) Chidyausiku.[1] The CCJP was approached for help by a number of people who had been disabled during the war and who received such paltry sums as Z$32, with the largest being Z$120. There were others who had been unable to access the fund at all. I subsequently gave evidence to the commission of inquiry on their behalf, but they received nothing further, as 'the coffers were empty'. The day after I appeared before the commission I received a phone call from one of the senior broadcasters with the Zimbabwe Broadcasting Corporation, who had interviewed me a few times previously and who was himself a veteran. He chastised me for about 20 minutes in a very loud voice for trying to prevent the 'War Heroes' from getting what was due to them from the War Victims Fund. Needless to say he never tried to interview me again after that.

During the commission hearings, proceedings were violently disrupted by 'war veterans' who invaded the High Court, where evidence was being heard, calling for an end to the inquiry. After order was restored the commission continued its work and reported to the President. The report was made public and disclosed that at least 117 people had benefited from the fund wrongfully and that the crimes should be prosecuted. The evidence was handed to the Attorney-General. Subsequently, some minor offenders were prosecuted, but the main offenders, including Reward Marufu, Mugabe's brother-in-law, who had received the highest payout from the fund (Z$800 000), were never prosecuted.

There were several other corruption scandals in the parastatal companies, notably the Grain Marketing Board, leading to Kumbirai Kanyai, the Minister of Lands and Agriculture and his Permanent Secretary being charged with corruption relating to the embezzlement of about Z$360 million. The case was a very long time coming to court and the result was a 'not guilty' finding for them both. Worse than this was the loss of Z$9 billion from the National Oil Company of Zimbabwe (NOCZIM) to corruption. The minister, Enos Chikowore, resigned, but he was never prosecuted.

Each corruption scandal was followed by the setting up of a commission of inquiry, but as soon as the culprits were exposed and found guilty Mugabe simply pardoned them. I began to realise that corruption had become a method of wealth redistribution to those who enjoyed his patronage and from whom he would in time demand reciprocation in one way or another. But still, in my mind at that time, the fault lay with those immediately responsible and not with Mugabe.

While I deplored the impunity that his friends enjoyed, I still found it possible to excuse him. I believed that he felt the need to balance the power structures of the party between linguistic groupings and party factions, and this made it impossible to dispense with the services of some of those party faithful whose corruption or poor performance would otherwise have demanded dismissal.

Another form of corruption altogether was Mugabe's handling of the war veterans, who became restive after the findings of the Chidyausika Commission were made public. On their return from the bush war, the ex-combatants of the various liberation movements had been either integrated into the National Army or demobilised with a pension of Z$200 per month for two years. At the time that amount of money was a good living wage. Some of the veterans saved their money, others went into business or found employment, but many simply wasted their assets and then sat back, feeling that the state owed them a living.

It should be remembered that the vast majority of Zimbabweans were involved actively in the war on one side or the other. Most civilians, particularly the rural women in the TTL, worked for the liberation forces – feeding, carrying, nursing, informing and caring for the fighters. Some could not actively join in the struggle, as they were detained at the time, which was the case for many of the nationalist leaders too. So it could be said that most people over about 10 years old in the early 1970s were war veterans. Several groups of war veterans had been formed, such as *Chimbwido*, the widows' association; Mujiba, the association of young boys who had carried messages for the guerrillas; and the former detainees association. But the main group was the Zimbabwe National Liberation War Veterans Association, made up of those who saw combat service. This group chose Chenjerai Hunzvi as its leader, the same Hunzvi who had helped people plunder the War Victims Compensation Fund, and the group was infiltrated by many people claiming to be war veterans but who were simply not old enough to have served in an active capacity.

The Association began in 1997 to press Mugabe and ZANU (PF) to reward their service to the nation satisfactorily. They claimed that many of their number were destitute because they had not had the opportunity to complete their education before going off to join the struggle. No doubt that was true in some cases, but most of the claimants were interlopers. After some rowdy demonstrations, the 'war veterans' rampaged through Harare and finished up by descending on the party headquarters and threatened to occupy them if their demands were not met. Although they made no formal financial demands, Mugabe stepped in and awarded them a package which included a Z$50 000 gratuity and Z$2 000 per month pension. At this time the average industrial worker was earning between Z$1 500–3 000 a month and farmworkers about Z$650 a month. Mugabe's gesture cost the country Z$4,2 billion immediately and an economist worked out that the whole package would cost Z$22 billion by the time the last pension had been paid. Of course, the payment had not been foreseen by the finance minister, nor had it been debated in Parliament. Mugabe was now acting on his own, using the Presidential Powers, to commit the country to this extortionate sum of money.

This was the first of three major blunders that were to spell disaster for the economy, for the ruling party and for the nation. The extraordinary wealth that had suddenly accrued to these veterans gave them an undeserved status in the country. They represented a new political force, closely aligned to the ruling party but sufficiently separate from it to be a threat; able to exert enough pressure to ensure the party's acquiescence in any demands they might make in the future.

Towards the end of 1997 the government announced that a new tax would be introduced in an attempt to finance the war veterans' payout. The mass of the ordinary people reacted strongly against this plan and a trade union-led work stoppage was held on 9 December. A demonstration planned for the same day was violently dispersed by the riot police despite the fact that two young lawyers, Tendai Biti and Brian Kagoro, had petitioned the High Court and been issued with a certificate allowing the demonstration to be held. It also forbade police interference in it. During the morning I was handing out copies of the court orders to various policemen, who were harassing demonstrators and ordinary pedestrians, and informed them that they were in contempt of court. This had little effect upon them.

I had positioned myself in front of the Parliament buildings in Mandela Street waiting for my son Michael to join me. A group of riot police occupied the corner opposite and as Michael approached they fired a tear gas grenade directly at him. Fortunately their aim was bad but he had to skip aside quite nimbly as it streaked past his ankles. They then moved us on with more tear gas which again was wasted. Later, in Second Street near the Anglican Cathedral, I had to come to the assistance of a young man who was in danger of being arrested because he had kicked a tear gas grenade back towards the policeman who had thrown it. We suddenly were surrounded by riot policemen threatening all kinds of mayhem. But then one of them accidentally dropped a tear gas canister at our feet, engulfing us all in the smoke. The policemen took off in one direction and the young man and I in another. When we had washed the gas off our faces at a nearby garage, we were able to see the funny side of the event and enjoyed a good laugh. At the garage we met Edwina and Newton Spicer, who were filming the proceedings. We joined them in their vehicle and as we continued to hand out copies of the court order to people still trying to assemble for the demonstration, we again bumped into the police, this time the uniformed

.....With 'friends' and a passing supporter outside the Anglican Cathedral.

..... Di gets involved.

branch. They told us that we could give the court orders to white people, but they said, 'not to blacks, because we will deal with them'.

On the day of the demonstration Mugabe was to deliver his State of the Nation address to Parliament. He was driven the two blocks from his office to the Parliament buildings through a totally deserted city. Although he knew of the running battles that had taken place that morning, in his address he made no mention of them at all. I found this bizarre. His behaviour confirmed my growing fears that the country had a dictator in the making.

The day after this demonstration I issued this statement on behalf of CCJP:

'The 10th December 1997 marked the fiftieth anniversary of the Universal Charter of Human Rights, which should have been the cause of universal celebration. Unfortunately, in Zimbabwe, that day was overshadowed by the grave violations on the previous day of the rights of Zimbabwean citizens in Harare by both the ZRP Riot Squad and the ZRP uniformed branch.

Members of the Commission eye witnessed the activities of the Riot Squad in the city centre, particularly the area of Africa Unity Square.

133

The Riot Squad, acting in violation of the law, and later in contempt of a High Court order:

- threw tear-gas without warning at totally innocent workers who had arrived for work;
- refused to allow citizens of Harare the freedom to move about their city, as is their right;
- cleared with tear-gas the vendors from the flower and craft stalls on the Jason Moyo side of Africa Unity Square;
- threw a tear-gas grenade at a newspaper vendor carrying out his legitimate business on Kingston's corner;
- fired tear-gas projectiles directly at any people gathered in the area, seriously injuring at least one person on the foot;
- fired tear-gas projectiles into buildings (for example Karigamombe and Eastgate);
- refused to allow any pedestrian to remain in any one place for any length of time;
- used batons and boots on any person who moved away too slowly.

The Commission condemns these actions in the strongest terms, as it condemns the vandalism and looting that took place in other areas, although it understands that this was caused indirectly by police action.

The Commission therefore calls on the Commissioner of Police to ensure that his force is aware of the laws of the land and/or the rights of the citizens, and that in future it will act to maintain law and order.'

In spite of the demonstration and the angry rejection of the new tax by the public, the government continued with the payout to the veterans, and the value of the Zimbabwe dollar plummeted. Although it appeared that Mugabe had bowed to pressure from the 'war veterans', I believe that he saw in them a new tool to use in maintaining his power. It was not long after this that the first invasions of white-owned commercial farms by 'war veterans' began in the Arcturus area, east of Harare.

Thus the second of Mugabe's three major blunders related to land designation. In November 1997 the Minister of Lands announced the designation of 1 400 commercial farms, and accordingly notified the 1 400 farmers. Under the 1992 Land Acquisition Act, government could purchase a designated farm, in its own time, and pay for the developments on the farm – but not 'for the land'. Payment for these developments was to be made over a certain period and would consist of both cash and government bonds. Naturally, this caused great concern to the farmers and to the investment community. News of the designation of these farms caused the value of the Zimbabwe dollar to drop once again, this time considerably. The economy of the country, which had shown some signs of improvement in the preceding couple of years, now began to totter seriously, jobs were lost, companies closed down and discontent grew among the people.

January 1998 saw the start of the food riots and the government showed that it was not against using the army to quell these disturbances. Using rifles and live ammunition, the soldiers shot dead at least 14 people and wounded many others. These expressions of public dissatisfaction, in the form of demonstrations or work boycotts, were to gather momentum and occur every few months, showing government's failing popularity with its people and requiring heavy-handed control by the police riot squad to contain the situation.

The third blunder came in July when Mugabe announced that he would send Zimbabwe's defence forces into the Republic of Congo to assist President Kabila in his struggle against the forces of Rwanda and Uganda. Once again, no budgetary arrangements had been made prior to this announcement, nor had Parliament been consulted, and it was obvious that this would be a most costly military adventure.

It was later also clear that although the cost to the nation was great, so was the wealth that accrued to ZANU (PF) and some of its members. Apart from the local business deals arising from this intervention, such as the contract for the transportation of military hardware to the Congo being awarded to a very senior army officer's transport company, diamonds, copper, cobalt and hardwoods from the Congo were as great a drawcard for the business interests within ZANU (PF) as they had been for the Belgian colonisers a century or so before.

CHAPTER 20

Morals and Hypocrisy

The fact that Mugabe could countenance so patent a rape of the resources of a country he purported to be saving from foreign interference motivated me to begin a careful study of the history of his party and his part in it. The more I delved, the more clearly I saw the relationship between Mugabe and violence. I remembered the pardons he had given to people who had committed grave crimes on his behalf. I noted the system of patronage and threats with which he maintained his power in the party. I saw, perhaps for the first time, the hypocritical face he showed to the world when currying favour and the threatening face he wore when a loss of political popularity and power loomed. I saw also that while Mugabe, his party and government often made good decisions and asserted that they were being implemented, on most occasions the reality did not match the rhetoric. They had become adept in obfuscation and for much of the time were ruling by confusion, so that nobody was very clear about what was happening.

I also began to look more closely at the continuing underdevelopment of Matabeleland and saw that the people of Matabeleland continued to be punished for their less than whole-hearted support of the ruling party. No effort had been made to compensate them for the atrocities committed during *Gukurahundi*. Although the report *Breaking the Silence: Building True Peace* had made clear recommendations with regard to the psychological 'closure' of the trauma suffered and to the development of the region, no action was taken on the recommendations until the run-up to the general election in 2000. During this period Mugabe set up a committee to look into paying compensation to individual victims, but needless to say, the committee did not even start work on the problem – the promise of compensation was just another election gimmick.

Early in 1995 Mugabe's private life and morals had come to the attention of the independent media. As he had no living children from his marriage to Sally, the photograph of a little girl attending the Dominican Convent, holding her suitcase with her name 'Bona Mugabe' painted on it (published in a news magazine), exposed Mugabe's affair with his secretary Grace Marufu. He had already had two children with her before his wife Sally had died. Angered by the press coverage, he seized the opportunity to shift the moral focus away from himself and onto gays and lesbians. The occasion was the Zimbabwe International Book Fair. Some time before the opening of the fair, the Gays and Lesbians of Zimbabwe (GALZ) had received permission from the fair organisers to exhibit their publications there. On hearing this, Mugabe refused to open the fair unless GALZ was banned. Having achieved this, he opened the fair with a scathing attack on GALZ and on homosexuals in general, saying: 'If we accept homosexuality as a right, as is being argued by the association of sodomists and sexual perverts, what moral fibre shall our society ever have? We don't believe they have any rights at all.' The hypocrisy of the man was extraordinary.

This episode, together with an earlier report in the *Financial Gazette* that Mugabe had married Grace Marufu in a small civil ceremony, must have persuaded Mugabe that he needed to regularise his relationship with her. He approached the Catholic Church to find a way around the facts that Grace was already married and had abandoned her husband and their children, and that he had been living in what, in the eyes of the church at least, was an adulterous relationship. The Archbishop of Harare found a way. Mugabe married Grace with full pomp and ceremony in August 1996, with the Archbishop of Harare officiating and other Bishops in attendance. The wedding is reputed to have cost about Z\$8 million. The marriage enraged the women of Zimbabwe, who had held Sally in high esteem, and cost Mugabe the political support of many of the women of the country.

This marriage brought Archbishop Chakaipa into a relationship with the President that lasted until the Archbishop died and almost silenced the voice of the Bishops' Conference for some years. The Archbishop had had a difficult time being the first black Bishop in a white-dominated church. He had become the Auxiliary Bishop of Salisbury in 1973 and had become the Archbishop in 1976 when the liberation struggle was at its height. He was an accomplished author and had often said that all he wanted to be was a parish priest so that he could continue his writing. His relationship with the CCJP had always been cautious and I believe that he thought the commission to be an unnecessary and abrasive part of the Conference, but he did acknowledge the work done. I suppose that he was a frightened man who did not want conflict in his life or in the workings

..... *Mugabe with Archbishop Chakaipa, firm friends*
to the end.

of the Bishops' Conference and he was aware that the work of the CCJP would necessarily entail such conflict within the church and the political arena. I believe it was this new relationship between Mugabe and the church, and more particularly between him and the Archbishop that led to the Bishops' Conference's continued refusal to approve the *Breaking the Silence* report.

The last social encounter that I had with Mugabe was at St Michael's Preparatory School. Tatenda, the younger of his two children, was in the same class as my grandson Clinton. Mugabe and his wife attended the prizegiving at the school that year, with Grace presenting the prizes, including one to my grandson for Environmental Studies. After the function, the parents and pupils gathered for refreshments in an adjacent hall. Mugabe caught my eye and brought his new wife over to introduce her to us. Di did not stay to meet her, however, as she held strong views about his relationship to Grace, having admired Sally very much. Mugabe was courteous and as friendly as always, and his wife was gracious, and then the brief moment ended. Again, I found it extraordinary that he should choose to treat me so civilly when we had been at political loggerheads for some time.

At about this time too I felt that an element of desperation had begun to touch Mugabe. As the world became less tolerant of dictators and sought to punish crimes against humanity through the International Court in The Hague, Mugabe no doubt realised that the human-rights violations that had taken place during his leadership of the country would certainly be considered sufficient for prosecution. In October 1998, when Augusto Pinochet, the former Chilean dictator, was arrested in Britain, Mugabe must have understood the danger that faced him if he were no longer a head of state.

CHAPTER 21

Crushing Dissent

A development in the 1990s that angered Mugabe and his party was the emergence of new independent newspapers. In the early 1980s, the only independent papers were the weekly *Financial Gazette* and the monthly *Parade* magazine, both of which tried to report objectively. In the 1990s Modus Publications, the owners and publishers of the *Financial Gazette*, launched the first independent daily paper, *The Daily Gazette*. Unfortunately, it could not compete with the national dailies in attracting advertising and had to close. The emergence of a new weekly, *The Independent*, in 1996 was a great boon to the Zimbabwean public as it was able to supplement the efforts of the *Financial Gazette* and carried excellent political commentaries.

Smith had tightly controlled the media in Rhodesia, particularly the radio broadcasting services, on which most people depended for news. It was used purely as a propaganda tool for the government and the ruling party. After the strict censorship of the Rhodesian Front regime, which was continued by the short-lived Muzorewa government, the early 1980s brought great relief to the journalists who could now report on news stories as they wished with very little control. However, the national daily newspaper publishing company, Argus Press, had been bought by government early in the 1980s and this had been through several phases of ever-increasing government control.

Not long after independence, individual government ministers found that the new-found press freedom exposed their mistakes and they began to demand 'responsible reporting', which meant that the journalists should report only positive news about the government and party. There ensued a period of self-censorship by journalists, caused by the fear of being sacked by government for 'unfriendly' reporting. The most notable victim of government displeasure was the inimitable Willie Musarurwa, who, at the time of his sacking, was the editor of the government-owned *Sunday Mail*. He had courageously attempted to tell some of the truth of what was happening in Matabeleland and was sacked immediately after the 1985 election. His sacking was interesting, because he had been sacked earlier in the same year by Nathan Shamuyarira, then the ZANU (PF) information secretary, but had been reinstated on Mugabe's orders. He later died of a heart attack in circumstances which, I thought at the time, were questionable.

Soon after this the government took great exception to both the *Financial Gazette* and *The Independent*, but was unable to find a way to close them down without causing an outcry. The two papers carried the independent press banner courageously for many years and continue to do so. Unfortunately, however, the average Zimbabwean could no longer afford to buy them. The only access they had to them was the old copies sometimes used as wrapping paper in rural stores.

A new and affordable threat to the government press emerged in the late 1990s. This was *The Daily News*, with Geoff Nyarota as its editor in chief. This newspaper appeared at a time when the government press had deteriorated further along the road of sycophancy, reporting nothing negative about the government and attacking the independent press at every opportunity. As *The Daily News* grew in popularity, so advertisers began to support the paper, despite government threats against companies and individuals who took their advertisements away from the national dailies. Many attempts were made to silence the independent papers, from the harassment of reporters and the arrest and detention of editors and publishers to the bombing of *The Daily News* office and its printing press.

These extraordinary crimes, reminiscent of the bombing of Mambo Press by the Muzorewa government in 1980, were never fully investigated and no one was ever brought to trial. The bombing of the printing press was obviously carried out by professionals as the destruction was complete, but the police simply made no effort whatsoever to investigate the case. Incredibly, but perhaps in an attempt to deflect suspicion, *The Herald* allowed its printer to produce *The Daily News* for a few days. But through all this, the newspapers' publishers and reporters continued to bring balanced news to the Zimbabwean public. In 2003, however, under new media legislation designed by Dr Jonathan Moyo, the Minister of Information, *The Daily News* was finally and forcibly silenced. Of Dr Moyo, more later.

The broadcast media were even more strictly controlled than the press as they were totally in the hands of party stalwarts and made no effort to conceal the fact. All political comment was carefully monitored and even when I and people like me were interviewed, the interviewers trod carefully around any controversial topic. Many of the political programmes broadcast on television were directly socialist in content and the broadcast was clearly intended to justify certain actions of government. One such programme, in the early days of the new nation, was 'The Road to Socialism', which was as propagandistic as one would expect in, say, Cuba. However, when it later became clear that as individuals the politicians of the ruling party were not inclined towards the principles of socialism, such programmes changed into plain propaganda for whatever the government was doing, had done or intended to do.

During the NCA constitutional education campaign (1998/99) it was decided to attempt to use the mass media to promote discussion of issues around the Constitution and to this end a set of television, radio and print advertisements were developed. In the initial stages *The Herald* and the ZBC were approached to flight the advertisements, which were aired very briefly and then stopped, on the instructions of the Minister of Information. The NCA then decided to embark on a different strategy in which it bought air-time in advance from the ZBC, for the airing of the nine programmes that would be titled 'Constitutional Talk'. The ZBC, on seeing the programmes, decided to air only three of them. The NCA then went to court to try to force them to honour their contract, but failed. It was in the light of this that it was felt that a challenge should be made to the state broadcasting monopoly. Thus Capital Radio was set up by my son Michael and his partner Jerry Jackson, who had been a broadcaster with Radio 3 and had become famous for opening airwaves to callers during the Food Riots of 1997, after she had been instructed to stop broadcasting. She was subsequently fired.

Capital Radio sought to establish that the state monopoly on broadcasting was contrary to the right to freedom of expression guaranteed under the Constitution, and thus sought to have the Broadcasting Act overturned, to enable private broadcasters to begin broadcasting. In October 2000 the Supreme Court (Constitutional Court) ruled that the state monopoly on broadcasting was illegal and that there was at that time '... nothing to prevent the applicant (Capital Radio) from proceeding with immediate effect to operate and provide a broadcasting service from within Zimbabwe'. At this stage Michael began to move his lodgings from friend to friend as he was sure that the police would begin searching for the instigators of this insolent court appeal; this nomadic existence served him well later, as they never did catch up with him.

Capital Radio set up its broadcasting station, and in the week after the Supreme Court ruling the first independent radio broadcast in Zimbabwe was heard. On that first day, the station theme tune was played and the station introduced. Capital Radio's first broadcast was from the roof of Mick Pearce's architectural offices, which later became the election offices of the MDC. Thereafter the station was moved to the roof of the popular hotel Monomatapa, and initially only music was played with Capital Radio backtrack. The police immediately set about searching for the station, but were totally frustrated for several days. Finally on the following Sunday a decision was made to broadcast the first discussion programme, on the newspapers and the stories they were carrying that day.

Fortunately, the hotel roof already held several radio and television masts so the Capital Radio mast was not too visible among them.

While the police search was proceeding, the directors of the company approached the High Court late one evening to seek protection for the very costly equipment that was being used; this protection was given in the form of an order preventing the police from searching the premises and confiscating the equipment. Despite this, however, Michael called me at about five the next evening to say that the police were in the hotel searching. I went down to see if my presence as a former head of the CCJP would be any kind of safeguard. However, while the police, in complete disregard of the court order, were dismantling and removing the equipment, we made sure that the company personnel were safe from the police. Once again the police showed absolute contempt for the courts as they had done so often before, and were to continue to do over the next few years, making a mockery of the judicial system that had been very well thought of throughout Africa and, indeed, the Commonwealth, for many years.

The police, having completed the removal of the equipment, then looked around for the troublemaking 'radio pirates' (to quote Jonathan Moyo, then Minister of Information), both of whom had long since disappeared from the scene. Before I arrived home later that evening Di phoned to say the police were at the gate looking for Michael; as they had no warrant she had not let them in. When I arrived they tried to persuade me to allow them to search the premises. I told them, 'it would be a pleasure to show you that neither my son nor his equipment are in the house, but as a Parliamentarian I have to stick to the law, and require you to produce a search warrant'.

They accepted this and remained camped outside our gate, on the pavement, for the remainder of the week. In the meantime other policemen were trying to find and search the other houses in which he had lived during the previous couple of weeks, but to no avail. For the following week, Michael and Jerry remained in hiding, and then launched another application in the Supreme Court to overturn the new Presidential Emergency Regulations, which the government had hurriedly put in place to ban the ownership of transmitters which would effectively nullify the previous order of the Supreme Court. Although the second case did reach the Supreme Court in 2002, by that time the issue of the broadcasting had become academic and Capital Radio donated its equipment to Radio

Dialogue, which was a studio set-up by Nigel Johnson, a Jesuit priest, to produce programmes on cassettes.

The second case in the Supreme Court was partly successful, but did not restore Capital Radio's right to broadcast and, at the time of writing, Capital Radio has a case before the African Commission for Human and People's Rights, supported by the Media Institute of Southern Africa (MISA) and Article 19.

Capital Radio was not the only broadcaster to have applied for a licence to broadcast at this time; the Catholic Church, through another Jesuit priest, Fr Oskar Wermter, had obtained finance to set up a training establishment and a small, local broadcasting station; the Munhumatapa African Broadcasting Corporation (MABC) tried unsuccessfully for some years to be licensed. When Capital Radio started broadcasting, another station, 100FM, led by Tich Mataz, a local celebrity DJ, also started broadcasting, but similarly stopped after a day or so.

The battle to open the airwaves in Zimbabwe is still being fought by the church, but the most important broadcasting for the country comes from Britain through a Zimbabwean group. Jerry Jackson subsequently set up a radio station in London called SW Africa which broadcasts on shortwave in the evenings and although SW is not easily accessible to all Zimbabweans it is the main source of external radio news for many. The Voice of the People broadcasts uses Netherlands-based transmission but has local journalists in Zimbabwe. Zimbabwean officials continue to attempt to jam these frequencies with equipment supplied by the Chinese.

CHAPTER 22

A Beginning and an End

Mugabe would brook no opposition. Over the years he had ensured that the opposition parties or politicians were silenced in one way or another; he had brought the universities under control; he had attempted to control the private voluntary organisations (with little success); he had kept the broadcast media and the national press on-side, as it were; and he was completely intolerant of opposition from within his own party. He was vindictive when dealing with internal dissent, but would keep those strongest in internal opposition beholden to him in whatever way possible. An example is his treatment of Eddison Zvobgo, probably the most learned man in his party. Zvobgo led the vaKaranga faction of the party; the vaKaranga were the people of Masvingo Province, the most populous province in the country, and its people among those who had made the greatest sacrifices during the struggle for independence. Zvobgo had always been a threat to Mugabe and since independence he had held one or other ministerial post. In 1990, he was demoted to Minister of Mines and subsequently dismissed from the cabinet. But Mugabe ensured his continued loyalty to the party by keeping him in the Politburo as the party's legal guru. Thus Zvobgo reverted to being a simple backbencher. He was a complex man and could have been a valuable opposition leader, but his loyalty to the party remained unshaken until his death in 2005.

The formation of the NCA and the publicity that accompanied it had created a great fear in the ruling party that power would be wrested from it if it did not control the process of building a new Constitution. Accordingly at the ZANU (PF) party congress of 1997 the party decided to drive this effort itself in order to ensure that it retained power and a resolution was passed to set this in motion. In March 1998, an MP from the Masvingo area, Dzikamai Mavhaire, was given the task of introducing the motion to Parliament. In his speech on the need to move ahead with constitutional change, he said, much to the consternation of Parliament: 'Mugabe must go.' (Mugabe must have been seriously offended by this retort as it so precisely echoed what his political opponents were saying.) This caused something of a furore, coming as it did from a supporter of a faction of the party that was feared by the leadership. Mavhaire was subsequently suspended from the party for a year.

During 1999 Mugabe gave Zvobgo the task of recruiting and planning the work of the proposed Constitutional Commission. Zvobgo invited the leadership of the NCA to three meetings to try to persuade us to join the commission and make our points through that channel. But ZANU (PF) would not allow him to accept the demands of the NCA concerning the composition of the commission or the programme it should follow. The NCA therefore remained outside the commission and continued to work on the Constitution. Zvobgo then tried to recruit some of us individually, he phoned me several times and in a most friendly voice told me how important it was to have the contribution of people like myself and how grateful he would be if I would join him. He said more or less the same words to several other members of the NCA, as well as others, including David Coltart. These efforts failed. Mugabe, however, went ahead and established the Constitutional Commission, under the chairmanship of Mr Justice Chidyausiku. Some 400 members were appointed to the commission, most of them ZANU (PF) apologists, including all the ZANU (PF) parliamentarians. It excluded all those who had introduced the topic to the nation and had been working so hard on it for the previous two years. There were, however, some respectable members of the commission, among whom were the former Anglican Bishop of Harare, Bishop Peter Hatendi and a former chairperson of the CCJP, John Deary, both of whom saw themselves as watchdogs for the process and who were most unhappy with the resulting proposals. By then it was clear that the end product was not going to satisfy the demands of those of us who were searching for justice and democracy.

The work of the Constitutional Commission ended rather abruptly in November 1999 after a meeting that was hurried through by the Chairperson to meet the deadline set by Mugabe. The meeting ended with several loud objections to the final draft and yet Chidyausiku claimed that the proposals he presented to Mugabe were arrived at by consensus. It was clear that many of the demands of the people had been ignored and that not all of the commissioners were happy with the proposals. Be that as it may, Mugabe accepted the proposals and promised to put them to the people at a referendum.

In September 1999 a new opposition party, the Movement for Democratic Change (MDC) was founded, based on the labour movements, which commanded a sizeable following in the country. The public acclaim at the launch of the party must have given Mugabe and his henchmen considerable cause for concern. The followers of this new party were by no means exclusively from the labour movements, as the desire to see democracy restored in the country was embraced by many people from civil society – the legal profession, business and agriculture. Many civil society actors left their organisations to join the new party as the situation in Zimbabwe was deteriorating obviously and rapidly; there was a great feeling of urgency to create change. It is a tribute to the citizens of Zimbabwe that civil society regenerated rapidly and later rallied under the banner of 'Crisis in Zimbabwe' to challenge the continuing excesses of the government. As the MDC grew in strength and put mounting pressure on government, so the civil society challenge mushroomed in both the urban and rural areas. The recording of human rights violations, the care for victims, the legal challenges and the demands for greater democracy all fell to civil society groups.

In the same year Mugabe himself had taken up the cudgels against the judges of the Supreme Court, who had written to him about the arrest and torture of the editor and a reporter for a Sunday newspaper, *The*

Standard, and the CCJP had issued a statement condemning the arrests and the actions of the Military Police, who had taken the journalists from police custody, detained them illegally for several days and tortured them severely. After their release I had arranged safe houses for them to allow them to recover from their ordeal. Mugabe, in his address, severely reprimanded the judges for their audacity in giving instructions, as he saw it, to the President:

> Their having done so can clearly be interpreted as an action of utter judicial indiscretion or as one of imprudence or, as I regard it, an outrageous and deliberate act of impudence.

He further implied that the journalists had received the treatment they deserved. This outburst against the judiciary was followed by a concerted attack over the following couple of years on white judges who wrote judgments that displeased the ruling party.

In the same speech Mugabe attacked Clive Wilson and Clive Murphy, the publishers of *The Independent*, as well David Coltart, a human rights lawyer, and me:

> The likes of Clive Wilson and Clive Murphy, complemented by the Aurets and Coltarts of our society, are bent on ruining the national unity and loyalty of our people and their institutions. But we will ensure that they do not ever succeed in their evil machinations ... Let them be warned, therefore, that unless their insidious acts of sabotage immediately cease, my Government will be compelled to take very stern measures against them and those who have elected to be their puppets.

It was with rather mixed emotions that I heard this outburst. At first I was somewhat amused that he found me a threat, but when what he had said sank in I became really angry. He was calling me a traitor, as the Belingwe police in the Smith era had done – the more I thought about it, the more outraged I became. Mugabe knew that my motivation in any work I had undertaken had always been in the national interest or in the interests of those who had suffered through the actions of his government. How dare he speak of me like that? It was now clear that Mugabe had realised that I would not countenance any human rights abuses; that in the path he had chosen, I would speak out against any and every attempt on his part or that of his government to conceal this.

Mugabe's speech was repeated in the broadcast media several times and featured prominently in the government press for several days. I did not believe that any official action would be taken against any of us, but several friends warned that Mugabe's words might be taken by some of his 'war veterans', the CIO or even the police as the go-ahead for some punitive action. I therefore requested protection from the Bishops' Conference. As my employers, they knew that I was not guilty in any way of the charges Mugabe had made. They were also aware of the injustice of the President's attack on Mr Justice McNally, a senior Catholic layman who had recently been appointed to the Pontifical Council for the Social Sciences, and on David Coltart, a deeply Christian person. I believed that it would be fitting for the Bishops to issue a statement in our defence. Neither as a Conference nor as individuals did they respond. This was to count heavily in my decision later to leave their employ.

The threatening attitude Mugabe had displayed in his speech was perhaps the final straw that broke any hold he had had on my feelings. I could see now what I had refused to recognise before – that Mugabe would brook no opposition at all to whatever plan he devised. He believed that he was the only person who had the right to engineer the future of the country. He would do anything that was necessary to maintain the power of the party and his own position within it. To this end he would pardon the most heinous crimes, he would accept the corruption of his party colleagues, and he would not concern himself with the torture and harassment used by his police and the CIO. He was indeed a most dangerous man.

At the administrative meeting of the Bishops' Conference in June 1999 the Bishops decided to change the image and *modus operandi* of the CCJP. They called for a new constitution for the commission, despite having approved our constitution only a year earlier. The minutes of that meeting, recording as they did some of the discussion during the meeting, showed clearly that the Conference wished to curtail the activities of the organisation, to place greater controls on the statements we would wish to make and to monitor the alliances we might wish to make with other organisations. Clearly they were thinking of the Legal Resources Centre, with whom we had produced *Breaking the Silence*, and the NCA, in which we represented the Zimbabwean churches views. I believed that particularly Archbishop Chakaipa, but also some of the other Bishops, were seeking to reduce the pressure the CCJP had maintained on the government, because of the new closeness between the church and the President brought about through his marriage and his apparently rediscovered faith. When I read those minutes I was extremely angry and the impact of the meeting, coming as it did after the Bishops' failure to offer protection after the Mugabe threats was the final cause of my resignation. The CCJP had stood for almost 30 years as a voice, sometimes the only voice, against the oppression and human rights violations of three regimes. That the Bishops who had established it now wished to silence it was simply too much for me.

As I left the CCJP I felt a deep sense of loss. It had been my life for so long and I had truly believed that what I was doing was good. But I also felt a growing anger against Mugabe. I believed that he was behind the pressure placed on me by the Conference, but mostly I was angry with him because what was happening in the country was unconscionable, tragic and disastrous. Now once again I was left with the problem of what to do with my life. I still had the work of the NCA, but the emergence of the MDC offered me a new way to continue to serve the country and, I hoped, the church.

CHAPTER 23

The Advent of the Unimaginable

As the year 2000 dawned the nation awaited two major political events: the constitutional referendum and the general elections due that year. There was a feeling of expectation, even excitement and certainly some anxiety, particularly among the young people – those who did not remember the war.

The two parties were now gearing up for these events, the MDC in a determinedly non-violent fashion and ZANU (PF) resorting to its tried and tested campaigns of violence, intimidation and propaganda. The national broadcast media, government vehicles and machinery became once again the exclusive tool of ZANU (PF). The ruling party campaign was augmented also by the 'war veterans' who saw the MDC as a threat to their newly acquired position in the party.

The announcement that the referendum would be held in February unleashed a storm of activity by both parties and the NCA, which had analysed the constitutional proposals accepted by the President and found them seriously wanting. These proposals would have the effect of simply entrenching the dictatorial powers Mugabe already exercised and retaining the majority of the skewed electoral laws.

At this stage another player appeared on the scene. Professor Jonathan Moyo, an academic who had been very critical of the ruling party for many years, but had spent some time out of the country, suddenly reappeared as the government's propaganda specialist and was given the task of persuading the people that they should accept the constitutional proposals. He had published a book in 1992 entitled *Voting for Democracy* in which he had been extremely critical of the electoral process in the 1990 elections; he had also criticised ZANU (PF) in many newspaper articles. His new position was in direct contradiction to his former stance, which might have been difficult to understand had he not left employment in both Kenya and South Africa in questionable circumstances. He may have seen a position of importance in ZANU (PF) as a way of saving himself a good deal of trouble and expense.

There was great excitement in the NCA when the referendum date was announced, as it meant that at last we had a real target to aim at; members of the organisation spread themselves all over the country trying to convince people that the constitutional proposals of the Chidyausiku Commission were seriously flawed and that a 'yes' vote would simply put them deeper in trouble. We assured them however, that a 'no' vote would allow the process to continue until we had the Constitution the nation deserved and desired. In this we were seriously mistaken, as will be seen from Mugabe's response to the result of the referendum. The feeling within the NCA was that we were involved in a sort of David and Goliath struggle in which the results were crucial to the future, and so great efforts were made to reach as many people as possible.

The NCA had no access to the broadcast media, but I think we were widely heard. The publicity team had produced thousands of T-shirts and posters and had even created a series of cassette tapes broadcasting our information from the tape decks of the emergency taxi fleets in the main cities. NCA workers both in the cities and in the countryside were exhorted to put 'a poster on every tree' and it must be said that they did their best. Meetings were held up and down the country with many great speakers, as the NCA had attracted a large number of lawyers, including an advocate, Welshman Ncube who was an eloquent if laconic speaker. Two other lawyers, Brian Kagoro and Tendai Biti, were powerful voices in the thrust for change. Other members such as Priscilla Misahairabwi, Grace Kwinjeh and Trudi Stevenson expressed women's point of view with strength and determination, and it was quite surprising that the message was well received even in most of the rural areas. On one occasion we even considered dropping leaflets from a light aircraft, but the expense and indeed the possible danger made us reject that particular idea.

The 'Goliath' of government, in the meanwhile, set up a campaign headquarters in the Harare Sheraton Hotel, with Jonathan Moyo, the disgraced academic, leading its campaign and creating a radio and television storm urging the people to vote yes. His group also produced T-shirts, posters and leaflets and again he had the machinery and funds of government at his command. We faced a massive challenge.

Less than a month was allowed for the campaigns for and against the proposals. The ruling party took it for granted that it would, once again, win the votes of the people. The NCA was, of course, given very little space in the national media to put its case, but it worked tirelessly with the MDC to inform the voters, and indeed the entire population, of the dangers of accepting so flawed a Constitution. Although several MDC and NCA members were arrested during the polling process, the referendum went off relatively peacefully, perhaps partly because there was a low turnout, with fewer than 30% of voters participating. The nation waited with bated breath for the results. The NCA staff and many of the members gathered in the office to listen to the results as they came in. The first results were depressing, as count after count produced a 'yes', but as time went by the 'no' votes began to come in and as the total rose so also did the hope and when the results were finally in, the shouts of joy almost lifted the roof off the office. Some 55% of those polled voted against the new proposals, signalling the first electoral defeat the party had suffered in 20 years.

Di and I were at a workshop she was giving for the staff of an NGO, in an hotel in Harare at the time, and the proceedings were held up for some minutes while we all celebrated. There was great jubilation throughout the country when the announcement was made. People were literally dancing in the streets. Hope for a new era was dawning. One thing that was very clear from the results was that the farmworkers and the farmers had taken part willingly and had voted a resounding NO!

The result was a stunning blow for ZANU (PF). Mugabe appeared on national television that evening, 12 February 2000. Although he was visibly very angry, he told the nation that his government accepted the result and respected the will of the people, with unfamiliar and unexpected humility (which later proved hypocritical). He said he took the defeat to mean that the people did not want a new Constitution – which was of course far from the truth. It was also clear that he saw the farmers' new interest in politics and the Constitution as a slap in the face, as he made a pointed reference to the participation of the white community in the referendum, saying, 'they have sloughed off apathy and participated vigorously in the poll'. Few whites saw this comment as in any way congratulatory, but did not realize what serious repercussions the results were to have. After the formation of the MDC he similarly harangued the white farmers for supporting what he called 'the British-driven and white-supported party' that was hoping to become the government of the nation. In his fury he had conveniently forgotten the enormous support his own party had received from the British people in his struggle for the country and the support his party had received from the people of Zimbabwe since Independence.

The Constitutional defeat was followed by an intensification of the violent farm invasions by the 'war veterans'. Already in 1998 the CCJP had received an anonymous letter warning of genocide against White settlers in Chimurenga III, as shown below. Now in 2000 Mugabe's plan for these

:.....*An anonymous letter warning of the farm invasions.*

people became clear. It must have been obvious to Mugabe and his party that they no longer commanded enough popular support to ensure their continued domination of power and of the people. It was necessary, therefore, to introduce a new element into the political scenario – the reclamation of the land from the colonisers.

The 'war veterans', who had already been involved, albeit a little half-heartedly, in the occupation of commercial farms, now took on the task with a vengeance. Within a matter of a day or so of the announcement of the referendum results, they invaded farms in the Masvingo province and, finding that neither the police nor any other arm of government objected, they moved on into other parts of the country. Soon their presence was being felt in most of the commercial farming areas. They proceeded to create a reign of terror in the farming areas, threatening farmers, farmworkers and their families. This was the beginning of the vengeful destruction of lives and livelihoods and the end of the relative economic stability of the mid-1990s.

As these attacks progressed without any police or government comment, they became more violent. Several farmers and farmworkers were murdered and others were beaten very severely; houses were ransacked and, on occasion, torched. Equipment was damaged, destroyed or stolen and many farmers were arrested for trying to resist this onslaught. They were never brought to court, however, but simply detained in the dreadful squalor of the police cells for a few days and then released.

Because I had spoken at so many farmers' meetings and Di had worked among the farmers and farmworkers in Mashonaland, we often had to answer phone calls from distressed farmers or their wives because their house was surrounded by shouting, drumming, often drunken men, and sometimes women as well, threatening mayhem if the whites did not leave immediately. Often the labour village had been visited first, and the workers beaten and chased away, most often with nothing but the clothes they wore. Unhappily we could not offer any help or even comfort, as the police in whatever area the raid was taking place paid scant attention to a phone call from miles away. In any case the behaviour of the Zimbabwe police force was disgraceful from very early in the independence era and it grew steadily worse. The cowardice of most of the policemen and women cannot be exaggerated.

This spreading of the 'veterans' over the country allowed the party to use them in the run-up to the general election due to be held before the middle of the year. Mugabe had left the announcement of the election dates as late as possible, but finally it was scheduled for 22–23 June. The ZANU (PF) election campaign that year was undoubtedly the most violent since Mugabe had come to power, with truly evil deeds committed by the followers of the ruling party. One could sense the desperation behind these actions and their absolute determination not to be unseated. For the party the consequences of a defeat were, in the words of John Vorster in another situation, 'too ghastly to contemplate'.

Early in 2000 I attended the first Congress of the MDC, which showed the national nature of the new party and the great hope it had raised among the people. I decided then that if I was asked I would agree to stand as a candidate for the party. In the event I stood for the Parliamentary seat of Harare Central at this election and during the weeks preceding the voting had to concentrate on my campaign. Fortunately there was little violence in the city centre, but my continued contact with the CCJP meant that I could keep the Director informed of the violence being perpetrated against the opposition party in other areas, as described later. The party and in particular its hierarchy knew then, as they know now, that defeat would mean the International Court in The Hague for Mugabe and his Fifth Brigade Commander, Perence Shiri. For most of his ministers and senior party officials it would mean prosecution for the corruption in most of the parastatal companies and in many ministries, as well as the loss of houses, land, vehicles and all their other ill-gotten gains. MDC had promised a 'national audit' in its election campaign, and assured the nation it would acquire the 'ill-gotten' property and sell it to recover some of the money stolen.

My own campaign, as with all other MDC campaigns, was a period of frenetic activity; as we had no access to television or radio, voters had to be

..... *Campaigning for election, 2000.*

visited or at least have the opportunity to hear the party policies at public meetings. I was fortunate in that my constituency was a city one and so did not have to deal with violence, as my rural counterparts did; they and their supporters were harassed throughout that period.

Di became my election agent, and my son Stephen took over the office manned by a number of party stalwarts, and appointed himself my bodyguard. He also provided, from his company, food for the workers when we had all-day meetings or door-to-door canvassing. It was an exciting but also a fearful time, as we were always aware of the great violence that was taking place in other constituencies. It was a time also when so many people offered assistance – financial, material and physical – with great goodwill and with the hope that change for the better could happen.

Now Mugabe began to show his true colours. He twice made death threats against the opposition and those who supported it. In a speech in Nyanga, he spoke of 'rivers of blood' if the opposition prevailed. Although he was speaking in chiShona at the time, the meaning was clear to all and his words constituted unmistakable intimidation. He continued to hurl a barrage of insults against the whites and against Britain and the Blair

..... *Cartoon relating to the 2000 election campaign.*

government. He described the MDC as a white-led party that would take the country back into colonisation and he insisted that what was happening on the farms was 'land reform', that he was returning the land to its rightful owners.

Mugabe campaigned tirelessly for his party. Every arm of government became a tool for the ZANU (PF) campaign and no expense was spared to improve its chances of winning the election. One such campaigner was the Registrar-General, Tobaiwa Mudede, a relative of Mugabe, who ensured that confusion reigned over who could or could not vote. The names of many white voters were removed, quite arbitrarily, from the rolls; people who had voted in all the elections to date were suddenly not entitled to the vote; the voters rolls were hopelessly out of date and featured a very large number of deceased people, and were not available to candidates until a day or so before the poll. Throughout the country people were subjected to grave intimidation and to beatings and the destruction of their homes. Teachers and nurses suspected of supporting the opposition were chased from schools, hospitals and clinics and lost their jobs. David Coltart's campaign manager was abducted days before the poll and has not been seen since. Several other MDC supporters lost their lives.

Perhaps I can best describe the horror of the campaign by quoting an extract from my maiden speech to Parliament a month or so after the election. My speech came after a remark made by Kumbirai Kangai, the ZANU (PF) MP for Buhera South:

It is unfortunate if the tactic of the honourable members on the other side is to create disorder in the country so that there is no investment which comes into the country ...

Which I followed with:

I would remind the Hon. Member that the particular disorder reigning in the country today began in February and has been allowed to continue unabated ever since. To my knowledge, no member of the ruling party has publicly condemned this peculiar brand of violent disorder, nor the people who have created it and who continue it still. Just a few nights ago, at a farm in Mazowe, several farmers were kept barricaded in the farmhouse by numerous, threatening and violent so-called war veterans. The police were there and, I believe, the riot squad, but by 9 pm they had done nothing to stop the criminal action; just a couple of nights ago, children were abducted and traumatised at a farm near Harare.

Let me be specific here. What we have witnessed since February has been the barbarism of the murders of Talent Mabika and Tichaona Chimini who were burned to death in their vehicle and, as was pointed out, in the full view of the police. What we have witnessed is the cold-blooded and wanton killing of David Stevens, the sadistic savagery of the murder of Martin Olds and the mindless thuggery which has killed some 35 other people before and after the election. What we have witnessed has been the brutality of the beating, torture and maiming of several thousands of other innocent people. What we have witnessed has been the abduction of many people and the death of at least two abductees. What we have witnessed is the burning and in some cases the total destruction of the homes of innocent people, including that of the Hon. Member for Kwe Kwe. What we have witnessed is not only the attacks on farmers and their workers, but attacks on teachers and health workers which deprives their pupils and patients of the services to which they are entitled as human rights. What we have witnessed, just last Monday, was the invasion by these miscreants of the offices of the Provincial and District Administrators in Gwanda referred to by my Hon. friend from Gwanda North, the disruption of their work and the destruction of files and furniture. What we have witnessed, Mr Speaker, Sir, is disorder of the gravest proportions caused, created, perpetrated and sanctioned by the ruling party. No, Mr Speaker, Sir, it is not the members on this side of the house who are causing or who intend to cause disorder in the country.

The election went ahead and several groups of observers arrived in time for the polling days which were, as always, relatively calm and peaceful. But few of the observers were willing to call the election free and fair because, quite apart from the violence, the national media had been closed to the opposition, the voters' rolls were unavailable and incorrect in many cases, and the reports of the violence were well documented by the human rights organisations, ensuring that the observers were well briefed on the situation during the campaign. I was fortunate to have a most enlightened woman polling official for the counting of the votes as, although my opponent from the ruling party had made little showing in the campaign period, we truly expected that the voting would somehow have been rigged (as the postal voting had already been) but our official allowed us to have as many observers as we wanted in the counting and watched the whole proceeding very carefully.

I won the Harare Central constituency by a fairly substantial majority. And when the counting and the celebration were over for us we waited nervously for the results of the other constituencies to come in. As our own win had been so substantial, hope for victory grew among my supporters and workers and, as the radio announcement of the results began

..... Newly elected MP for Harare Central.

our joy was almost overwhelming. The urban counts were the first to be completed and the MDC won seat after seat of the first twenty or thirty to come in and each win raised a huge cheer that must have been heard in the next city. However, as the results began to trickle in from the rural constituencies, the ZANU (PF) stronghold, we began to see victory fading.

The result of the election was a great shock to ZANU (PF). The MDC won 57 seats and ZANU Ndonga (the party previously led by Ndabaningi Sithole) retained the Chipinge seat it had held since 1980. ZANU (PF) won 62. This meant that the opposition had won four seats, less than half of the elected seats in the House. But there were still 30 seats to be allocated by the President to his lackeys. Nevertheless, the result was a great victory for the MDC, not only because of the seats won but also because its followers, despite the intimidation, beatings and other violence before the poll, had voted in substantial numbers and had almost brought off an electoral defeat for the ZANU (PF) monolith.

I was one of four whites who won seats; the others were David Coltart, who had worked with me to produce the *Breaking the Silence* report, Trudi Stevenson, a civil rights activist and Roy Bennett, a farmer from Chimanimani who had been harassed for some time. We became the target

..... *In the House with Trudi Stevenson.*

of the anger of Mugabe and his party, who insinuated that we would steer the country back to colonisation because we were 'British agents'.

At the opening of the new Parliament, when Mugabe arrived to inspect the guard of honour, his arrival was greeted with a barrage of the open-hand sign of the MDC and deafening chants of *chinja, chinja, chinja* (meaning 'change, change, change', from the MDC slogan *Chinja maitiro* – Change direction), which could be heard even over the sound of the military band playing for the occasion. As we took our seats in the House for the first time to listen to his opening speech, I felt a surge of hope that the opportunity for us to expose ZANU (PF)'s misrule and challenge its excesses had arrived and might well lead to a change of government at the next election. Di and David's wife Jenny were in the parliamentary enclosure and felt the same great surge of hope that affected us all. They showed the open hand to Mugabe as he passed, to the annoyance of the ZANU (PF) wives who were also in attendance. That morning the MDC members all appeared in Parliament wearing black armbands in memory of those who had died during the campaign.

As Mugabe left the House after his speech, he and I looked at one another for a brief instant and I could see only enmity in his eyes.

CHAPTER 24

Hope Dies

I attended Parliament for the following 18 months, During this time I maintained close contact with the CCJP, the LRF, Amani Trust and various other organisations, including the CFU, the Farm Orphan Support Trust (FOST) which cared for children affected by AIDS, the National Employment Council for the Agricultural Industry (NEC Agric) by whom I was employed as a consultant, and the Farm Community Trust of Zimbabwe (FCTZ), which, like NEC Agric, kept me in touch with the farmworkers and their union. These contacts were invaluable as they kept me aware of the developing situation in various sections of the population.

The President announced his new cabinet and it was noteworthy that the ministries that were to become critical to the future path of the government were given to unelected members. Justice, Legal and Parliamentary Affairs went to Patrick Chinamasa, who had previously served as Attorney General; Information went to Jonathan Moyo and Lands and Agriculture went to Joseph Made, an incompetent man who could be easily manipulated. These three people were to play central roles in the land and governance debacle that was to follow.

The first months of the new Parliament had the appearance of normality. Motions were put, debates ensued, divisions were won or lost. Parliamentary portfolio committees were formed and started work on their allotted tasks and parliamentary work seemed to settle into a routine. But it was when Bills were presented that the most obvious result of skewed democracy became apparent. The ruling party, despite having only a tiny majority of the elected seats, now used the Chiefs and the 20 appointed MPs to ensure that whatever Bill the government wished to force through would be passed. It soon became obvious that eloquence in debate, truthfulness, logic and genuine concern had no meaning for the ZANU (PF) members in the House. No matter if, as individuals, some of them were persuaded of the dangers of whichever Bill was being debated, when it came to the vote, if the government wanted to pass a Bill, no one on the government side of the House had the courage to vote against it. In addition, the ZANU (PF) government had long been adept at saying the correct thing, and either doing the opposite or doing nothing at all. Perhaps the best example of this related to a motion I put to the House in October 2000 'that this House calls upon the government to sign and ratify the UN Convention against Torture'.

Over the years torture had been the topic of much correspondence between the CCJP and various ministries – Defence, Home Affairs, State Security and Foreign Affairs – but always without meaningful response. So, having gained a seat in Parliament, I again brought up the subject. Before I introduced the motion, I distributed copies to MPs of the 1987 CCJP document entitled 'A Report on the practices of Torture and Brutality employed by members of the Security Services of Zimbabwe in the investigations of Criminal, Subversive or Political activities of citizens of this country'. I wanted to ensure that all the MPs were aware that these practices had been and still were being used, as had been shown by the torture of two journalists in January 1999. The motion was seconded, but thereafter there were no contributions to the debate until I closed it some months later. When the motion was put to the vote it was accepted by the House without a dissenting vote. One would have expected, therefore, that the government would proceed to sign the Convention and ratify it. This did not happen and when I asked the Leader of the House, Patrick Chinamasa, some six weeks later, when we could expect it to happen, he thanked me for reminding him about it and assured me that the process would be started. To date, nothing has been done to carry out what was ostensibly the unanimous instruction of Parliament to the government. The reason is clear. ZANU (PF), through the partisan police, security services and the 'war veterans' continue to use torture systematically against the people considered to be opposition supporters.

As the year 2001 unfolded, it became increasingly clear that Mugabe and his government intended to continue with their version of land reform. The presidential election was due before June 2002 and there was grave concern among the members of the ruling party that the MDC candidate for the Presidency, Morgan Tsvangirai, would win the election unless something could be done to regain the support of the people. The government believed that by promoting the land grab as 'the return of the land to the people from whom it had been stolen in the past' this could be achieved.

Here three ministers – Chinamasa, Moyo and Made – became the front line. Chinamasa as Justice Minister and Leader of the House was to introduce the necessary legislation, new or by amendment; Moyo was to use the state media to distort the truth or to broadcast lies, repeatedly, and to attempt to offset the truth told by the independent newspapers and the foreign media; and Made was to implement the programme, using the 'war veterans' as his tools. These three therefore became far more important to the party than they would otherwise have been, considering that they were relative newcomers to the hierarchy and that, in all three cases, their presence in Parliament was by appointment rather than by popular vote. There is no doubt that many of the older members of the politburo were unhappy with the rise of these three upstarts.

As the year 2001 wore on it became obvious that although the MDC Parliamentarians were far superior in the debates and were able to bring the truth into Parliament, we were not likely to have any major effect on the government benches. The ZANU (PF) members were simply not listening to the truth or to the logic of our arguments; their task was to ensure that if government wished to win any vote in the House they would follow their whip and their majority would prevail. The business of voting became almost a game for the ZANU (PF) backbenchers, many of whom knew little of what was happening and understood less, but they would treat the vote as a kind of soccer match and crow about the 'numbers they scored' compared to ours, whenever a division was called.

One thing that became increasingly clear to us was that ZANU (PF) members were very adept at deflecting blame onto someone else for whatever went wrong. Often Britain or America, the whites in general, the Smith government or the judiciary were blamed; never once did we hear the government admit that it had made any mistakes. This brought a touch of humour to one particular debate when my colleague and friend Paul Themba Nyathi, an MDC MP, told the House that if 'ZANU (PF) opened its legs and smashed a rock down on its manhood, it would blame the rock for the emasculation'. After a moment of stunned silence, the remark brought the house down.

There was, however, one advantage to our debating contributions that made our efforts worthwhile: the independent and foreign media knew the truth of what was happening in the rural areas and reported on it. This was a continuing thorn in the flesh of the government, and led the state propagandists to redouble their efforts to bring more and more distortion and confusion into the picture.

Draconian new security legislation was promulgated that outdid even the reviled Law and Order (Maintenance) Act in its oppressive measures. Continual adjustments were also made to the Land Act and its various regulations as the farmers took their cases to court and had their complaints upheld. But as the courts ruled more and more often against the government, so the pressure on individual judges mounted. The government seemed to be determined to rid the courts, and perhaps especially the Supreme Court, of the judges who had served with such courage and integrity over the years.

In mid-2001, the 'war veterans' demonstrated at the Supreme Court and threatened the Chief Justice, Justice Anthony Gubbay, who was still several months away from his official retirement date. They continued their demonstration at his home, where his wife lay terminally ill. This led to his early retirement, leaving the position of Chief Justice open for

Chidyausiku, a lackey of the party who, as a judge of the High Court, had had his judgments questioned on many occasions. His appointment, against the advice of the Law Society, meant that the government had in place a malleable Chief Justice who would do all in his power to ensure that his decisions pleased Mugabe and his henchmen.

However, the pressure on the remaining independent judges remained high, especially from the Minister of Justice, who continually decried them in the House. He accused the judges of questionable judgments, of supporting the farmers rather than the government, of racism and of being British. By this time the British Government, and in particular Prime Minister Tony Blair, had become Mugabe's favourite whipping boys, along with the white farmers and the MDC MPs, so to be accused of being British was to be called a traitor. This led to my family placing the following advertisement in one of the independent papers:

SUPPORT THE JUDICIARY

Michael Snr, Diana, Peter, Stephen and Deanne, and Michael Auret, firmly supporting the rule of law and the role of the judges, who for so many years have courageously upheld the laws created and accepted by the people and Government of Zimbabwe, condemn in the strongest terms the bullying attempts of the Minister of Justice, Legal and Parliamentary Affairs to purge the judiciary of the moral and principled judges of the Supreme Court.

We mourn the loss of respect for the truth in our country, and we urge the good people of this country to support wholeheartedly the judiciary and to hold them and the nation in their prayers. We pray that our country and people will soon enjoy the justice and peace we deserve.

Evil cannot prevail over good

Unhappily, later in the year Justice Ibrahim resigned from the Supreme Court, and in December Mr Justice McNally retired. Three new judges were appointed to this highest court, which was also the Constitutional Court, thus ensuring that it would in future be sympathetic to government.

After the opening of the second session of this Parliament in July 2001, it became clear that the House was to be used only to pass undemocratic and oppressive legislation. The MDC members were not to be allowed to tell the country or indeed the world the true state of affairs in the country. When Parliament sat to debate the new measures, the opposition debate was simply drowned out by the raucous shouting from the government benches, making it impossible even for the Hansard writers to hear and report it correctly. As the Speaker and his deputy were ZANU (PF), they did little to control the behaviour of that side of the House. Clearly, neither the government nor its party wanted to hear the truth told and it became impossible to have a serious debate on any matter.

This state of affairs caused me great stress. I discovered that whenever I sat in the House I became very angry, to the extent that I had difficulty formulating responses to whatever debate was in progress, especially when I knew that a particular ZANU (PF) Minister or MP was lying. To give an example of the extraordinary ability of the ruling party for telling lies, I asked a question of the Minister, Joseph Made, about the well-being of the farmworkers who had been displaced by the 'land grab', and he responded with a direct lie, then left the House. He was a man I had known for many years; a brother of his had served with the JPC during the Rhodesian days. Some time later I met him in the lobby of Parliament and said:

'Joe, you are not telling us the truth, are you?'

To which he replied:

'I know, Mike, but what can I do?'

I was angered by the seeming impossibility of achieving anything when the truth was so wantonly abused. I was angry at the frustration of knowing that even in Parliament we were unable to affect the well-being of the nation. I have always disliked anger, and now this enormous anger made me unwell.

Suddenly I found I was tired – tired of living behind 6-foot walls, electrified fences, protected windows and having a 24-hour guard; tired of watching my rear-view mirror whenever I drove anywhere and worrying constantly about my family.

I left the country to seek medical attention in South Africa in 2001. I did not resign my seat immediately, as I knew that the Presidential election was due the following year and I wished to lead the constituency in that vote. I returned to Zimbabwe for the election and was not surprised to find that though I was still an MP, I was no longer on the voters roll in my constituency. I was allowed to vote finally after appealing to the Election Directorate. I finally resigned my seat in June 2003.

Robert Mugabe appeared on the world stage in 1980 as a man of great intellect, a pragmatic and progressive leader. To the people of Zimbabwe he appeared as a saviour who had rid the country of oppression; who was magnanimous in forgiving the past and who would lead the country to a peaceful and prosperous future. Aside from the Matabeleland terror, much of which was hidden from the nation, great things happened in that decade. The second decade saw what appeared to be the corruption of the man by the power he had arrogated to himself, and as the decade progressed so that corruption seemed to have become absolute. The arrest of Augusto Pinochet and, perhaps, the attempt by Peter Tatchell to arrest Mugabe, must have caused him to consider the possibility that he was in danger of arrest if he were no longer the President. The arrest and trial of Slobodan Milosevic must have reinforced that feeling of danger. In those circumstances it became necessary to ensure absolutely that he could not be defeated through the electoral process.

That Mugabe is corrupt cannot be disputed. It is evident in the wealth he has amassed; in the fact of his adultery; in the abuse of his Catholicism in silencing the church while ostentatiously practising the faith; in the violence of his 'clean-up' campaign to rid the cities of the opposition voters; and in the hate-filled diatribe he aims at all those who oppose him, even senior members of the church.

For my part, I spent the first decade believing in him, despite Matabeleland, and working hard to bring about the development he seemed to want for the country. In the second decade, disillusionment began and the drive for development became a drive for democracy and the protection of human rights. But it became clear as time went on that a

white person who considered himself indigenous and who dared to criticise would not be accepted in an authoritarian state. The ZANU (PF)
newspaper *The People's Voice* once wrote a disparaging and totally untrue
article about me and my past and, although it published a front page apology, and a letter from my children a few weeks later, the feelings that had
caused the paper to write the article in the first place were deeply sadden-
ing and worrying. Although I had always hoped that things would change
for the better, the new century and the continued destruction of that wonderful country and so many of its people, left us no alternative but to leave
and seek peace elsewhere. We have found that peace, security, friendliness
and great kindness in Ireland, where we now live.

As we drove away finally from our country, I remembered the dream
– the euphoria of 1980, the enthusiasm with which we returned to help
complete the transformation of the nation to one in which all had life and
hope, where the land, all land, became productive and industry flourished
and people were happy and secure. There was a deep bitterness when I
remembered all Mugabe had done to his enemies and even to some of
his friends. I remembered the reasonable man and wondered if he had
changed or if indeed he had always been so evil, but simply more adept at
hiding it. I remembered his friend Didymus Mutasa saying in Parliament,
and on several other occasions, when a member of the MDC had spoken about the many thousands of people dying of AIDS-related illnesses,
'I don't care if there are only five million people left as long as they are all
ZANU (PF).' Yet this is a country of 13 million people.

Was he corrupted by his leader or was the whole story of the struggle
for democracy and human rights simply a means to a wealthy and powerful end?

No, I could not have stayed any longer.

Epilogue

In September 2002, Mugabe attended the World Summit on Sustainable Development, held in South Africa. He was applauded by some sections of the audience for his speech in which he railed against Britain and scoffed at the 'smart' sanctions. He boasted of his 'land reform' but did not mention that between one and two million people had left his country searching for a better life, a life that his style of land reform cannot provide. He did not mention the many thousands of people tortured, starved and made homeless, or the hundreds of thousands dying prematurely of AIDS aggravated by malnutrition and lack of treatment.

South Africa, the country that had supported Smith and the Rhodesian Front, although finally forcing them to accept majority rule, now supports Mugabe. Despite the good intentions of the SADC and the aspirations of the New Partnership for Development (NEPAD) and its insistence on good governance, no country in Africa by mid-2008 has done anything to assist the people of Zimbabwe or to unseat this tyrant who has deprived his people of their basic civil, political and legal rights.

Mugabe attended several Southern African Development Community (SADC) summits between 2003 and 2006 and was acclaimed at each of them. In Mauritius he signed the SADC protocol on free and fair elections but continues to ensure such elections are impossible in Zimbabwe, without comment from his SADC partners.

Perhaps Mugabe has carried out the vengeance against the colonists that the Mau Mau in Kenya, the people of the Belgian Congo and Idi

Amin in Uganda have tried. Perhaps that is what Africa wants. But perhaps, despite the enormous harm he has done to his people in achieving it, he will go down in African history as the man who 'returned the land to the people'.

Whatever the case, the spirit of the people of Zimbabwe will never be crushed. They have suffered much for so many decades with only brief periods of peace and they have survived. They will come through this terrible time with new heart and a new direction, and perhaps will ultimately lead Africa away from nationalist politics and towards democracy, justice and peace.

Appendices

1. Chronology

1890	Colonists arrive
1893–5	First *Chimurenga* (resistance)
1953	Federation established
1960	Independence for the Congo
1963	ZANU established
1963 (December)	Federation dissolved
1964	Ian Smith becomes Prime Minister
1972	Onset of war
1976	Patriotic Front is established
1978	Salisbury Agreement
1979	Muzorewa forms government of Zimbabwe-Rhodesia
1979 (September)	Lancaster House talks begin
1979 (December)	Agreement is reached
1980	First full elections
	Mugabe become Prime Minister
1983	*Gukurahundi* begins
1987	Unity Agreement signed
1992	Land Acquisition Act promulgated
1997	Farm invasions begin
1998	NCA established
1999	MDC established

2000 (February)	Constitutional referendum
2000 (July)	General Election; MDC wins 57 seats
2002	Rigged Presidential elections
2006	President for Life?

2. Place names

Current	*Previous*
Zimbabwe	Rhodesia
Harare	Salisbury
Chinhoyi	Sinoia
Mutare	Umtali
Masvingo	Fort Victoria
Gweru	Gwelo
Shabani	Zvishavane
Kwe Kwe	Que Que
Esigodini	Essexvale
Marondera	Marandellas
Hwange	Wankie
Kadoma	Gatooma
Chegutu	Hartley
Nyanga	Inyanga

3. Acronyms and abbreviations

Bde	Brigade
CFU	Commercial Farmers Union
CHOGM	Commonwealth Heads of Government Meeting
CIO	Central Intelligence Organisation
DC	District Commissioner
FCTZ	Farm Community Trust of Zimbabwe
FOST	Farm Orphans Support Trust
JPC	Catholic Justice and Peace Commission
LRF	Legal Resources Foundation
MDC	Movement for Democratic Change
MIO	Military Intelligence Officer

MP	Member of Parliament
NCA	National Constitutional Assembly
NEC	National Employment Council
NEPAD	New Partnership for Africa's Development
NOCZIM	National Oil Company of Zimbabwe
NRR	Northern Rhodesia Regiment
OSB	Officer Selection Board
PF	Patriotic Front
RBC	Rhodesia Broadcasting Corporation
RF	Rhodesian Front
RLI	Rhodesian Light Infantry
RENAMO	National Resistance Army of Mozambique
SLR	Self-loading rifle
SADC	Southern African Development Community
SCF (UK)	Save the Children Fund (United Kingdom)
TTL	Tribal Trust Land
UDI	Unilateral Declaration of Independence
UN	United Nations
UNIP	United National Independence Party
ZANLA	Zimbabwe African National Liberation Army
ZANU	Zimbabwe African National Union
ZAPU	Zimbabwe African Peoples' Union
ZIPRA	Zimbabwe Peoples' Revolutionary Army

Index